Topics in Context

Global Perspectives

Cornelsen

Topics in Context Global Perspectives

Im Auftrag des Verlages herausgegeben von
Prof. Hellmut Schwarz, Mannheim

Erarbeitet von
Barbara Derkow Disselbeck, Köln
Allen J. Woppert, Berlin
sowie
Angela Ringel-Eichinger, Bietigheim-Bissingen
Geoff Sammon, Bonn

in Zusammenarbeit mit der Englischredaktion
Hartmut Tschepe (verantwortlicher Redakteur); Neil Porter;
Dr. Ilka Soennecken (Bildredaktion); Cornelia Hansch (Redaktionsleitung)

Design und technische Umsetzung
Petra Eberhard Grafik Design, Berlin

Gestaltung des Lead-ins
Anette Schamuhn, Berlin

Umschlaggestaltung
Klein & Halm Grafikdesign, Berlin

Dieses Themenheft wurde auf der Grundlage des Kapitels *Global Perspectives* des Oberstufenlehrwerks *Context 21* entwickelt.
Das *Teacher's Manual* (ISBN 978-3-06-032902-1) enthält eine Audio-CD und eine DVD-ROM/Video (mit den Videos zum Schülerheft, interaktiven Tafelbildern für Whiteboard und Beamer, Vorschlägen zur Leistungsmessung und weiteren Materialien).

1. Auflage, 1. Druck 2011

Alle Drucke dieser Auflage sind inhaltlich unverändert und können im Unterricht nebeneinander verwendet werden.

Druck: CS-Druck CornelsenStürtz, Berlin

ISBN 978-3-06-032885-7

Inhalt gedruckt auf säurefreiem Papier aus nachhaltiger Forstwirtschaft.

adj	adjective
adv	adverb
AE	American English
BE	British English
cf.	confer, see
e.g.	(Latin) exempli gratia = for example
esp.	especially
etc.	(Latin) et cetera = and so on
ff.	and the following lines/pages
fig	figurative(ly)
fml	formal
i.e.	(Latin) id est = that is, in other words
infml	informal
jd./jdm./ jdn./jds.	jemand/jemandem/ jemanden/jemandes
l./ll.	line/lines
n	noun
p./pp.	page/pages
pl	plural
sb.	somebody
sl	slang
sth.	something
usu.	usually
v	verb

CD 04 indicates that the listening text(s) can be found on the audio-CD in the Teacher's Manual (Track 4).

DVD indicates that the video(s) can be found on the DVD-ROM/video in the Teacher's Manual.

IWB indicates that interactive material (for use with an Interactive Whiteboard or a projector) can be found on the DVD-ROM/video in the Teacher's Manual.

EXTRA indicates additional (optional) materials and tasks.

Webcode: TOP328857-9

is a code that can be entered at www.cornelsen.de/webcode.
This connects you directly to a specific website related to a section of this book.

Oxfam* indicates that the word, expression or name (here: *Oxfam*) is explained in the Glossary on pp. 44–47.

☆ indicates that the American English pronunciation follows.

Global Perspectives

International thinking at its best!

Question: What is the truest definition of Globalization?

Answer: Princess Diana's* death.

Question: How come?

Answer: An **English** princess
with an **Egyptian** boyfriend
crashes in a **French** tunnel,
driving a **German** car
with a **Dutch** engine,
driven by a **Belgian** who was drunk
on **Scottish** whiskey,
followed closely by **Italian** paparazzi,
on **Japanese** motorcycles;
treated by an **American** doctor,
using **Brazilian** medicines.

This is sent to you by an **American**,
using Bill Gates's technology,
and you're probably reading this
on your computer,
that uses **Taiwanese** chips,
and a **Korean** monitor,
assembled by **Bangladeshi** workers
in a **Singapore** plant,
transported by **Indian** lorry-drivers,
hijacked by **Indonesians**,
unloaded by **Sicilian** longshoremen,
and trucked to you by **Mexican** illegals ...
That, my friends, is Globalization.

3 **How come?** Why?
22 **plant** factory
25 **Sicilian** *(here)* Americans of Sicilian descent
longshoreman person who loads and unloads ships at a port

1 IWB **Talking about the poem**

a Use a map to identify the places named in the text and draw lines between them in the order in which they are mentioned.

b What do you think is the intention of the poem? Explain how its tone is appropriate for the intention.

c EXTRA Which areas of the world are missing from the text? Think what they might be able to contribute, e.g. natural resources, and add two more lines to the text with two new nationalities.

d Which aspects of globalization are mentioned in the text? Start a mind map on aspects of globalization. Find words and phrases in the text, and add more as you go through this book.

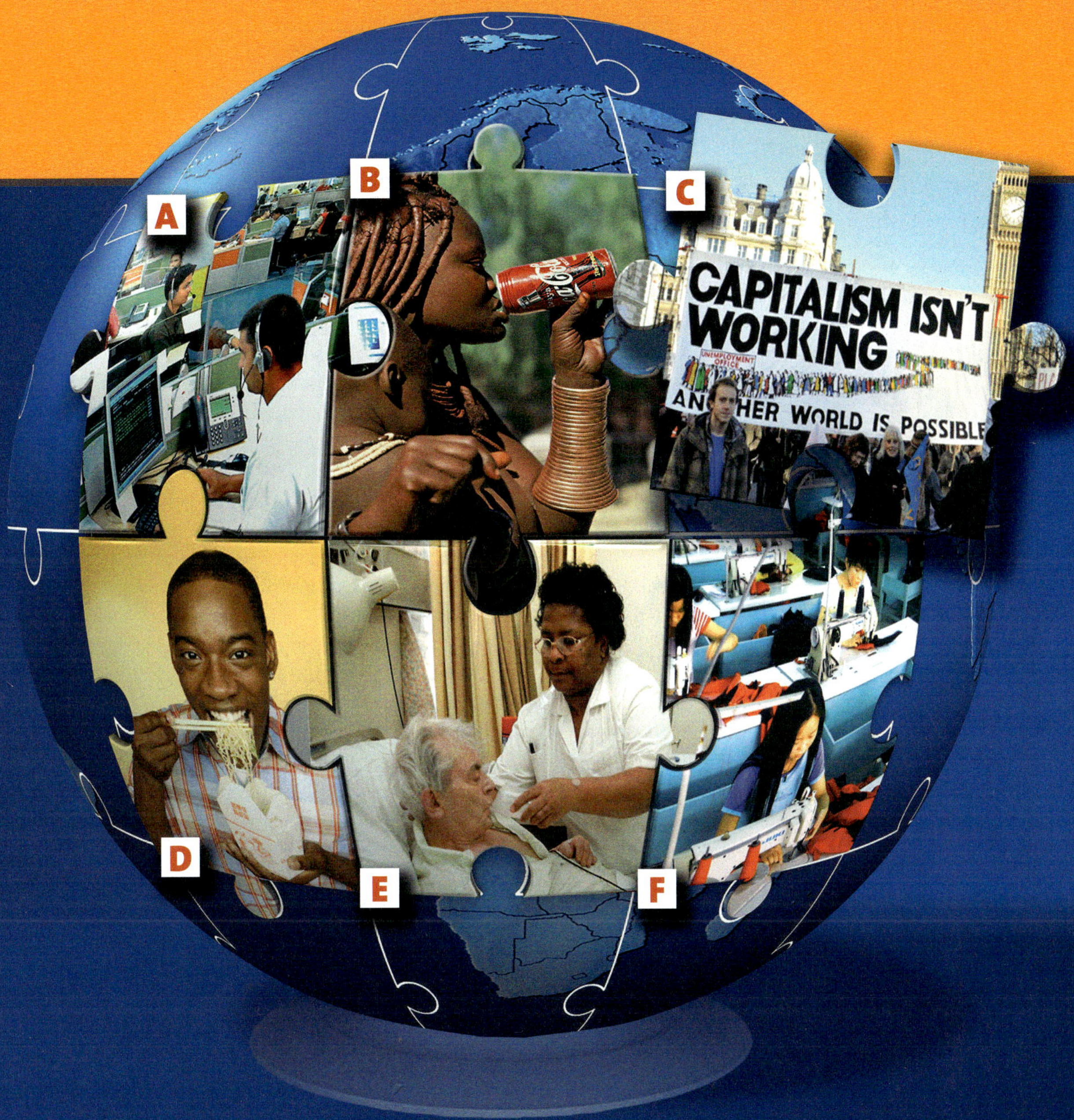

2 IWB Talking about the photos

a Describe each photo and explain how it relates to the title of this book.

b Explain how photo **C** might be seen as a response to some of the other photos.

c On your map from **1a**, mark the places where you think the photos above might have been taken. Speculate on what other country might be linked to that place through a person or product in the photo. Mark and link the two places on the map.

d Compare and discuss your map with a partner. ■ **Language help**

e Write captions for the photos. You can add and write captions for other photos related to aspects of globalization and put them all in your portfolio.

Language help

- I think photo A may have been taken in a ... in ...
- I agree/disagree. I marked ... because I think ...
- the women are making ... / the woman is drinking ...
- a product for ... / from there

Everything Is Connected

The word 'globalization' usually refers to the breaking down of trade barriers between nations. For supporters of globalization the deregulation of trade and the elimination of national protectionism are positive things: without trade barriers, goods can pass freely from one part of the world to another. In this way people in developing countries get access to world markets. At the same time the competition between companies allows the consumers in developed countries to buy goods at lower prices. The market forces of supply and demand regulate prices.

To globalization critics, free trade comes at the expense of workers in developing countries. They work long hours, often in unsafe or unhealthy conditions in so-called sweatshops, where they barely earn a subsistence wage and do not enjoy job security. These factories often use child labour. Trade unions try to organize workers and improve working conditions, but these attempts are often met with violence.

At the same time, skilled and unskilled workers in the developed world feel that they too are victims of globalization. Their employers compare production costs of plants at home and abroad and conclude that domestic production is too costly. Jobs are then outsourced to a developing country with a huge labour force. These employees are willing to work for considerably lower wages.

Consumers can occasionally affect the way workers are treated in developing countries. Under threat of boycotts by concerned consumers, some multinational companies, especially in the garment industry, have committed themselves to 'ethical manufacturing'. A brand's image is important to the company, so it will do its best to avoid bad press. Therefore some companies encourage the countries from which they import their goods to protect the rights of their workers. Many globalization opponents avoid big brands altogether and buy 'fair trade' products made by workers who receive a fair wage and work in a safe and healthy workplace.

One result of globalization is that – figuratively speaking – the world is getting smaller. Individual countries are more dependent on the global economy than ever before. Just how interdependent the world is became evident in the financial crisis which began in 2008, when bank failures and the bankrupting of entire industries were only prevented by government intervention.

International trade is regulated by the World Trade Organization* (WTO), which encourages free trade. WTO summit meetings as well as those of other economic institutions such as the Group of Eight* (G8, eight industrialized countries from the northern hemisphere) are targets for lobbying and protests.

Besides the organizations that try to regulate the world's economy, there are international bodies that look after other aspects of international relations. The United Nations* (UN), for example, deals with health issues, the problems of refugees and, of course, national and international conflicts through its peacekeeping missions*. Elsewhere in the world, the European Union*, the Commonwealth* and others work to provide security, peace and stability. Most relief efforts in impoverished countries or disaster areas are carried out, however, by so-called 'non-governmental organizations'* (NGOs) such as Médecins Sans Frontières* or Oxfam*. Although they receive some government funding, these organizations rely largely on donations and volunteer work.

1 Words in use: Comprehension

a Match words and phrases from the two boxes that mean the same or about the same. Those in the left box are taken from the text on the opposite page.

- *break down trade barriers*
- *deregulation*
- *earn a subsistence wage*
- *enjoy job security*
- *globalization opponents*
- *labour force*
- *outsource*
- *improve working conditions*
- *domestic production*
- *peacekeeping mission*

- *anti-globalization activists*
- *make just enough money to survive*
- *manufacturing at home*
- *relaxing of laws*
- *be safe from unfair firing*
- *operation to maintain peace in a conflict zone*
- *send jobs abroad*
- *stop protectionism*
- *make workplaces better*
- *workers*

b Write sentences with four words or phrases from each box. Remember to add new words and phrases to the mind map which you started in the Lead-in (p. 6).

2 Dictionary work

Complete each sentence with a noun, verb or adjective formed from one of the words on the right. You may need a dictionary to find the right words.

bankrupting · consumer
critic · developed
employee · opponent
regulate · supporter

1 The president has been highly ... of business people who receive huge bonuses although their job performance has been rather poor.
2 The economic crisis which followed the collapse of the financial market drove a number of companies into ...
3 The trade union issued declarations that were ... of the workers who went on strike.
4 The United States ... approximately one fourth of the annual world oil production.
5 Because of globalization, people with foreign language skills have a better chance of finding ... than those who speak only their native tongue.
6 People who ... globalization are often portrayed as naive or as hypocrites in the mainstream media.
7 The aim of the new government is to promote economic and social ...
8 The government has asked for new ... powers over banks to make sure that another financial crisis does not occur.

3 EXTRA Activate your vocabulary

Translate the following sentences. Pay special attention to the underlined expressions. Look at the text again if necessary.

1 Billige Lebensmittel sind für uns eine gute Sache, aber sie gehen auf Kosten der Arbeiter in den Entwicklungsländern.
2 In den meisten Entwicklungsländern haben die Beschäftigten lange Arbeitszeiten und keinen sicheren Arbeitsplatz.
3 Die Arbeiterinnen haben kaum ausreichend Geld, um ihre Familien zu ernähren.
4 Protestaktionen gegen Wirtschaftsgipfel wird oft mit Brutalität begegnet.
5 Das globale Finanzsystem ist, im übertragenen Sinne, ein Kartenhaus, das zu jeder Zeit kollabieren könnte.
6 Im In- und Ausland setzen sich Aktivisten für Menschen ohne Mitspracherecht ein.

Webcode: TOP328857-9

▸ Further Practice 1–3 (p. 26)

Case Studies in Globalization

A1 The Price Make-up of a €100 Sport Shoe

Adapted from www.cleanclothes.org

1 Comprehension

Find the correct price in the illustration of the shoe for each of the following parts of the production process.

1 the cost of mass production in a factory or sweatshop
2 the tax added to the shoe when it is sold to the customer
3 the cost to the company selling the shoe of renting a shop and keeping a choice of shoes ready for the customers
4 the money spent on shop assistants
5 the money given to the worker who makes the shoe
6 the money the company selling the shoe spends on advertising
7 the money the company whose name is on the shoe has made after everything is paid for and the shoe is sold

2 Reaction

Explain what surprises you most about the different figures. Discuss whether this sort of information would influence your choice of brand.

3 Expressing information in different ways

► Skill 1: Working with charts and graphs (p.32)

a Make a chart to display the information from the illustration. Remind yourself of the different sorts of charts and what they best display. Explain your choice of chart for this task.

b Discuss with a partner which you find more effective – the chart or the illustration – and why.

Webcode: TOP328857-10

A2 The Jeans Kelsey Timmerman*

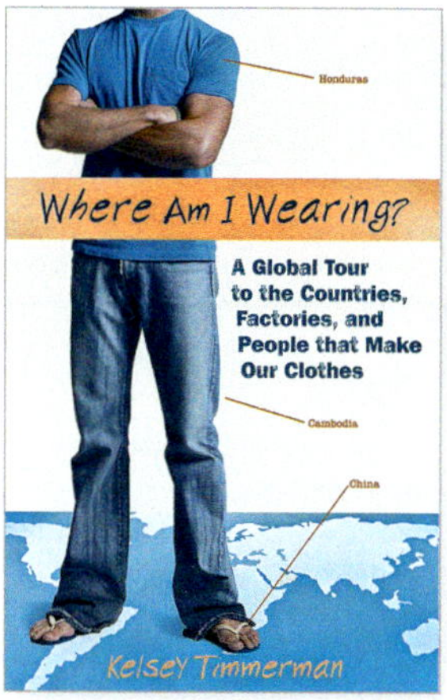

Timmerman is a freelance writer who decided to find out about how and where the clothes he wears are made. So he set off on a global tour. In this extract from the book that he wrote about his experiences, he is in Cambodia.

I spot Nari in the crowd and offer to treat her and the other girls to lunch. I've got a lot of questions to ask them, including one very important one.

Nari turns down my offer of lunch and leads me back to the apartment where the stove is already fired up and lunch is on. Phoan and Chendu cook away.

Pork, rice, green beans, some salad, and I'm full. Phoan offers me more rice, and I feel obligated to take it. I sit on the floor and go at the bowl with my spoon, wondering if I'll ever see the bottom. [...]

'When you're done,' Nari says giggling, 'you can do the dishes.'

'Where are you girls from?' I pull out my notebook and start in with questions.

Most of these girls are from rural areas outside of Phnom Penh. They miss their families and life in the village, but had to move to the capital to find work. They send part of their monthly wage home to their families.

'How much do you send home?' I ask Chendu.

'$7.50 per month,' she says. That seems like a pretty high percentage since she only gets paid $45 per month.

'How about you?' I turn to Phoan.

'I make $60, and I send home half,' she says.

'Geez,' I joke, 'I want to have you as my daughter.'

Phoan gets real serious, 'I support 10 people. I have five brothers and five sisters. I have no education. I can't do anything else but work at a garment factory.'

The room falls silent.

'What would you tell someone in the USA who won't buy the jeans that you make because they don't think you are paid enough or treated fairly?' I ask.

Phoan, lost in thought, stares at the floor.

'If they pay $45 for jeans,' Ai says, 'it helps us. If people don't buy, I'm unhappy because I wouldn't have a job.' Ai laughs at the simplicity of the logic.

Is it that simple? Does an uneducated, 24-year-old garment worker hold the answer to how I should behave as a consumer?

To buy or not to buy, that is the question.

[...] A British documentary uncovered child labor at factories producing for GAP and Nike in 2000. Both companies, having been subjected to the bad press that fell upon many global sourcers in the mid- and late-1990s, pulled out of Cambodia. Thousands of Cambodians lost their jobs, and a budding industry was threatened. But factories, unions, and international organizations worked hard to correct the industry's problems and now market the industry as sweatshop free.

Today, Ai is lucky to work for one of the most monitored garment industries in the world. With organizations such as the International Labor Organization (ILO) protecting Ai's rights, they are, in turn protecting the big brands' images, and our consumer conscience.

It's a powerful thing, our pocketbooks. We should use them wisely.

From: *Where Am I Wearing? A Global Tour to the Countries, Factories and People that Make Our Clothes*, Hoboken/NJ: Wiley 2009

1 **treat sb. to sth.** jdm. etwas spendieren
3 **turn sth. down** refuse sth.
6 **feel obligated to do sth.** feel you have to do sth.
8 **be done** *(infml)* have finished
10 **rural** of/from the countryside
17 **make sth.** earn sth.
18 **geez** [dʒiːz] wow!
19 **support sb.** provide money for sb.
20 **garment** piece of clothing
32 **pull out of sth.** leave sth.
33 **budding** *(adj)* growing
36 **monitor sth.** watch sth. carefully
39 **conscience** [ˈkɒnʃəns] Gewissen
40 **pocketbook** *(AE)* wallet

1 Comprehension

Summarize the text, pointing out briefly and clearly the argument Timmermann introduces in ll. 30–39.

► Skill 5: Writing a report (p. 35)

> **Tip**
>
> A **news story** (or news item or news report) gives a report of recent events of general interest that appear in newspapers. A news story usually addresses the five w's: Who? What? Where? When? and Why?

2 Writing a news story

a Rewrite the text as a news story entitled 'Changes in Cambodian Factories'. First check that you understand what a news story consists of.

b With the definition of a news story in mind and using your answer from **1** above, choose six of the nine facts below that you should include in your news story.

1 the fact that the girls eat at home
2 the fact that the girls come from rural areas and have moved to the capital
3 the fact that they send part of their wages home
4 the amount of money they earn
5 the number of people in Phoan's family
6 the fact that clothing companies left Cambodia due to the bad press about child labour and bad conditions
7 the fact that the Cambodians corrected the industry's problems with the help of international organizations
8 the fact that Ai is happy to have a job in a clothes factory
9 the fact that the girls work in clothes factories monitored by international organizations

c Choose one of the following sentences to start your news story.
Discuss why you chose yours and rejected the others. You can, however, write your own opening sentence.

1 The garment industry in Cambodia has changed in a way that allows Westerners to buy clothes with a good conscience.
2 Ai and Phoan moved from rural areas of Cambodia to the capital to earn money.
3 Many people in the West buy clothes made by poor people in developing countries.

d Now write your news story in about 150 words.
How would you end your story? You could choose your own ending, or you could base your conclusion around Timmerman's last sentence.

► Skill 2: Taking part in a discussion (p. 33)

3 A class discussion

Divide the class in two: one half prepares arguments for, the other against consumer boycotts. Find a partner with the opposite view and discuss the issue.

4 EXTRA A class survey

Do a class survey to find out where everybody's clothes are made and where the headquarters of the companies responsible are based.
Use charts to present your findings.

► Skill 1: Working with charts and graphs (p. 32)

Webcode: TOP328857-12

► Further Practice 4–5 (p. 27)

A3 DVD Outsourcing

▶ Word Help (p.43)

- **Before watching**
  Many companies have relocated their telephone call centres to developing countries. Why do you think this might be? What advantages and disadvantages are there to the company, the workers and the customers?

EXTRACT 1 'Eight heads for the price of one'

At the start of the film Outsourced*, *Todd is the supervisor of the telephone sales section of a US company with a very good MPI record (minutes per incident – an incident being a sale).*

1 While watching
a What does the company sell?
b What changes are there going to be, and why?
c Explain why Todd accepts the job in India.

2 After watching
Do you think Todd is going to enjoy his stay? Why (not)?

EXTRACT 2 'It's a culture thing'

Todd tries to teach his Indian team that language and cultural attitudes play a big role in telephone sales.

1 While watching
a What does Todd want the Indians to do?
b What is Asha's problem with his instructions?

2 After watching
a Summarize Asha's point about the English language.
b Do you find it easier to understand Todd or the Indians?

EXTRACT 3 'It's impossible!'

After three weeks Todd's team is doing well. Then his boss Dave turns up unexpectedly.

1 While watching
Point out how Asha persuades the American customer to buy the company's goods.

2 After watching
a Explain why the problem that arose could be solved quicker in India than in the USA. Think of: improvisation, rules and regulations, health and safety rules, personal commitment to one's employer, working hours.
b Explain why Dave says 'China is the new India'.
c Compare the effectiveness of the film with that of the texts you have read so far in helping you understand globalization. Illustrate your answer.
  ▪ **Language help**.

Language help
- The atmosphere / background information in the film/...
- It's easier / more difficult to identify with the characters
- you can understand a big issue when you can see ...
- the impact on an individual's life

The Globalized Economy

B1 Global Money, Global Crisis

Thomas L. Friedman

It's easy to move money around the globe. Big companies and banks have been doing it for years, and nowadays ordinary citizens do it too. But moving money around the world has its risks, and those risks are often hard to see, as this examination of the international financial crisis of 2008 shows.
As you read the text, add words and phrases that have to do with money and finance to the mind map you started in the Lead-in (p. 6).

If you're looking for a single example of how the globalization of finance helped get us into this mess and how it will help get us out, you need look no further than British newspapers last week and their front-page articles about the number of British citizens, municipalities and universities – including Cambridge – that are in a tizzy today because they had savings parked in Icelandic banks, through online banking services like Icesave.co.uk. [...]

When I went to the Icesave Web site to see what it was all about, the headline read: 'Simple, transparent and consistently high-rate online savings accounts from Icesave.' But then, underneath in blue letters, I found the following note appended: 'We are not currently processing any deposits or any withdrawal requests through our Icesave Internet accounts. We apologize for any inconvenience this may cause our customers.'

Any 'inconvenience'? When you can't withdraw savings from an online bank in Iceland, that is more than an inconvenience! That's a reason for total panic.

So what's the story? Around 2002, Iceland began to free its banks from state ownership. According to *The Wall Street Journal*, the three banks that make up almost the entire banking system in Iceland 'grew quickly on easy credit' and 'their combined assets rose tenfold in five years.' The Icelandic banks, while not invested in U.S. subprime mortgages, had gone on their own borrowing and lending binges, wooing savers from across Europe with 5.45 percent interest savings accounts.

In a flat world, money can easily seek out the highest returns, and when word got around about Iceland, deposits poured in from Britain – some $1.8 billion. Unfortunately, though, when global credit markets closed up, and the krona fell, 'the Icelandic banks were unable to finance their debts, many of which were denominated in foreign currencies,' *The Times* reported. When depositors rushed to get their money out, the Icelandic banking system had too little reserves to cover withdrawals, so all three banks melted down and were nationalized. [...]

So think about it: Some mortgage broker in Los Angeles gives subprime 'liar loans' to people who have no credit ratings so they can buy homes in Southern California. Those flimsy mortgages get globalized through the global banking system and, when they go sour, they eventually prompt banks to stop lending, fearful that every other bank's assets are toxic, too. The credit crunch hits Iceland, which went on its own binge. Meanwhile, the police department of Northumbria, England, had invested some of its extra cash in Iceland, and, now that those accounts are frozen, it may have to reduce street patrols this weekend.

And therein lies the central truth of globalization today: We're all connected and nobody is in charge.

From: 'The Great Iceland Meltdown', *The New York Times*, 18 October 2008

4 **municipality** [mjuˌnɪsɪ'pæləti] town or city
be in a tizzy be nervously excited or confused
10 **deposit** [di'pɒzɪt ☆ -'pɑːzət] putting money into a bank account
withdrawal [wɪð'drɔːəl] taking money out of a bank account
11 **inconvenience** [ˌɪnkən'viːniəns] Unannehmlichkeit
18 **asset** something of value that a person or company owns
19 **subprime mortgage** ['mɔːɡɪdʒ] Hypothek, die an wenig Kreditwürdige vergeben wurde, was der Auslöser der Probleme für viele Banken war
binge [bɪndʒ] short period of excessive, uncontrolled behaviour
20 **woo sb.** [wuː] try to attract sb.
23 **krona** currency of Iceland
24 **debt** [det] Schulden
be denominated in foreign currency auf ausländische Währung lauten
29 **credit rating** Einschätzung, ob jd. ein Darlehen zurückzahlen kann
30 **flimsy** weak
32 **toxic** poisonous
37 **in charge** responsible

1 Understanding the text

a Fill in the flow chart to explain how Britons lost their money in Iceland (ll. 15–35). The words you have added to your mind map will help you.

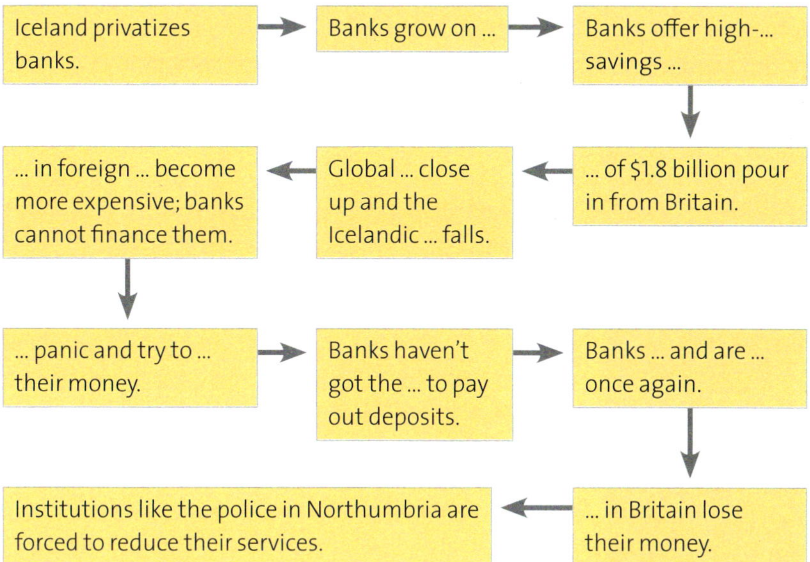

b Explain the completed chart to a partner. Use past tenses. ▪ **Language help**

c EXTRA Look again at ll. 28–32. Use the facts there to make your own flow chart showing the roots of the banking crisis.

Language help

- X resulted in ... / led to Y
- X ..., which was followed by Y ...ing ...
- As a (direct) result/ consequence (of X), Y ...
- Because of this, ... / For this reason, ...
- When X ..., Y ...
- Consequently/Therefore, ...

2 Language work

a Paraphrase the following expressions to show what they mean. Use a dictionary if necessary.

1 'consistently high-rate ... savings accounts' (l. 8)
2 'withdraw savings' (l. 13)
3 'banks ... grew quickly on easy credit' (l. 17)
4 '5.45 percent interest' (l. 20)
5 'money can ... seek out the highest returns' (l. 21)
6 'finance their debts' (l. 24)

b EXTRA Make sentences with the money and finance terms from **a**, but leave a gap for the words. Exchange papers with a partner, who then completes your sentences.

IS THAT JUST FOR THE NIGHT, OR FOR EVER?

3 Examining the text

a Analyse whether the last sentence of the article is justified by what has gone before.

b Show how the text is divided into three parts: introduction, body and conclusion. Give line numbers. Identify the signals the writer uses to indicate where each new part begins.

▶ Skill 3: Structuring a text (p. 34)

▶ Further Practice 6 (p. 28)

> ⚠ **Trouble spot**
> **effect** *(n)* = (Aus)Wirkung
> **affect sth.** *(v)* = etwas beeinflussen

B2 EXTRA The Butterfly Effect Thomas Hylland Eriksen*

Thomas Hylland Eriksen is a Norwegian professor of anthropology who often writes about academic subjects for non-academic audiences.
Before you read the following extract, use your dictionary to find out what sort of work anthropologists do. What might that have to do with globalization?

The culinary capital of India may be London, that of China San Francisco. In order to carry out anthropological fieldwork in a village in the Dominican Republic, one has to spend at least a few months in New York City. The little trolls, 'Scream' t-shirts and expensive knitted sweaters sold to tourists visiting Oslo are made in Taiwan, Pakistan and Sri Lanka, respectively. The largest city in the English-speaking Caribbean is London. And [...] when shops in California (and elsewhere) have to close down because their customers have lost their jobs, this is partly a result of competition from East Asia.

Such is the extent of global interconnectedness – and I still haven't even mentioned satellite television, the Internet, cheap flights and cellphones. Some theorists compare the complex webs of connectedness in the current era to chaos and complexity in physics [...], mining complexity theory for models that can be used to understand social change.

The most famous image from chaos theory* is that of the butterfly effect: A butterfly flapping its little wings on the Brazilian coast whips up some air and changes the direction of a tiny wind. This wind connects to other streams of air, changing parameters in the atmosphere ever so slightly for each step, and one of the cumulative effects is, say, a blizzard in Maine. The reasoning behind the butterfly effect is old as the hills, as witnessed by this familiar English rhyme:

> For want of a nail, the shoe was lost;
> For want of the shoe, the horse was lost;
> For want of the horse, the rider was lost;
> For want of the rider, the battle was lost;
> For want of the battle, the kingdom was lost;
> And all from the want of a horseshoe nail.

The general point here is that small changes can have momentous effects, or rather, that tiny variations in the initial parameters of a process may, through complex feedback processes, lead to major differences in the outcome. Now, 'butterfly effects' as such are rarely observed in globalization processes, but the point is rather that in a steadily more interconnected world, the distance between cause and effect is often enormous. Space is relativized; urban Trinidadians may feel that Barbados and even Miami are closer than Mayaro in rural Trinidad, and although you exercise little power over your neighbour, you may work in a company with the power to hire and fire people in a Malaysian town.

From: *Globalization: The Key Concepts*, Oxford: Berg, 2007

5 **troll** in Scandinavian mythology, a giant or tiny creature that looks like an ugly person
'Scream' reference to a famous painting by Norwegian artist Edvard Munch (1863–1944)
7 **respectively** in the order mentioned
12 **extent** Ausmaß
16 **mine sth.** *(here)* look deeply at sth. in order to find something useful
22 **parameter** [pəˈræmɪtə] something that limits the way something else can be done
23 **cumulative** [ˈkjuːmjələtɪv] resulting from everything that has gone before
26 **for want of sth.** because sth. is missing
shoe *(here)* horseshoe (= Hufeisen)

1 Comprehension

Define the butterfly effect in your own words.

2 Examining the text

a Explain the examples the writer cites in the first paragraph of the extract and their function in the text.

b Relate the butterfly effect to the rhyme (ll. 26–31).

3 Beyond the text

a Look at the following photos. With a partner, decide in which order the events of 12 April 2004 probably took place. ▪ **Language help 1**

b Take it in turns to present your scenario to two new partners.
▪ **Language help 2**

power restored · L.A. air traffic control still affected

L.A. airport · without power · emergency lights

bird · power pole near L.A. · transformer · short circuit

flights out of L.A. · delayed up to 90 minutes

air traffic · disrupted · chaos

power plant · shut down · ten seconds

Language help 1

- I think / I'm pretty sure the bird landing / ... has to come first/next.
- X could have caused Y.
- No, I think X is the result of Y. Look, ...
- Don't you think it makes more sense if ...?
- I think that's a cause, not an effect.

Language help 2

- When ..., it caused ...
- This in turn led to ...
- The resulting ... meant that ...
- It took a few minutes/... to ...

4 Creative writing

Invent your own 'butterfly effect' chain of events, e.g. 'How the fact that a man in Freiburg couldn't get to sleep one night resulted in the loss of 1,000 jobs in Beijing'. Write it in the form of a report.

Webcode: TOP328857-17

► Skill 5: Writing a report (p. 35)
► Further Practice 7–8 (pp. 28–29)

B3 Global Protest Kevin Danaher*

Dr Kevin Danaher co-founded the anti-globalization activist group Global Exchange. In this text he examines the global economy.

Globalization of market forces creates greater inequality.

Over the past 30 years the globalization of the economy – led by the World Bank*, the International Monetary Fund and transnational corporations – has proceeded at a quickening pace. These institutions have pressured governments to remove barriers to the cross-border flow of money and products. Also, advances in telecommunications and computer technology have made it possible for trillions of dollars in finance capital to zoom around the world, 24 hours a day, searching for the highest rate of interest.

> ⚠ **Trouble spot**
>
> a million 1,000,000
> a billion 1,000,000,000
> a trillion 1,000,000,000,000

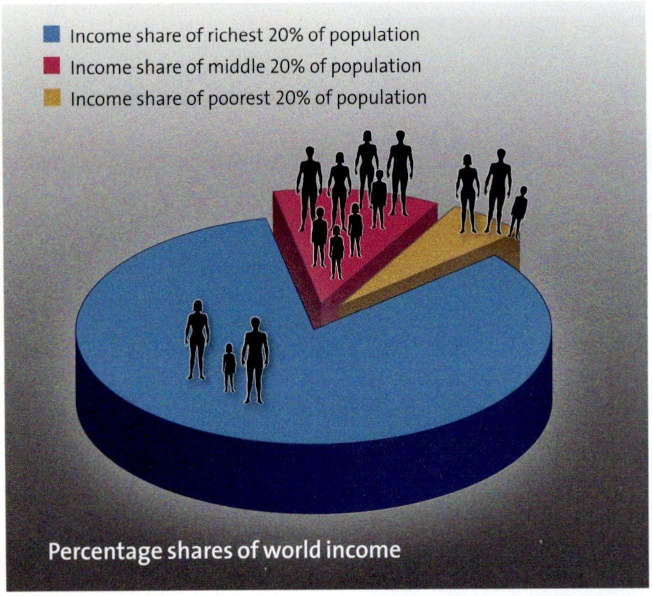

Percentage shares of world income

This globalization of market forces has greatly increased the inequality in the world. [...] Now the richest 20 percent of the world's population receives 83% of the world's income, while the poorest 60% of the world's people receive just 5.6% of the world's income. The richest 20% of the world's population in northern industrial countries uses 70% of the world's energy, 75% of the world's metals, 85% of the world's wood, and 60% of the world's food. This 20% minority is also responsible for producing about 75% of the world's environmental pollution. [...]

The system is being rejected by millions of people all over the world.

Globalization-from-above is controlled by wealthy elites and driven by a hunger for more wealth and power. But there is another form of globalization made up of grassroots alliances of human rights activists, trade unions, women's organizations, environmental coalitions and farmers' organizations. This 'globalization-from-below' does not get as much publicity as the elite form of globalization but it is growing just as rapidly.

This bottom-up form of globalization does not have the amount of money or guns possessed by the elites but it does have moral authority. Just think about the contrast between the dominant system's focus on greed and our focus on meeting human needs.

This alternative vision calls for more openness and accountability by institutions such as the World Bank, the IMF* and transnational corporations. It calls for raising wages, health and safety standards in the third world to bring them up to first world levels, rather than driving first world standards downward in a desperate effort to keep capital from fleeing to lower wage areas. It calls for stewardship of natural resources that will preserve something of the environment for our grandchildren to enjoy. It seeks to redefine self-interest so that it is more in line with the common interest of humanity.

The choice confronting us today is which of these two global visions we prefer.

From: 'Seven Arguments for Reforming the World Economy', website of Global Exchange, 28 October 2007

4 **at a quickening pace** at a speed that is getting faster
5 **advance** *(n)* progress
20 **reject sth.** [-'-] etwas ablehnen
23 **drive sth.** etwas (voran)treiben
25 **grassroots** at the level of ordinary people
29 **rapid** ['ræpɪd] fast
34 **call for sth.** demand sth.
accountability Pflicht, Rechenschaft ablegen zu müssen
38 **flee (fled – fled)** leave quickly
stewardship of sb./sth. ['stjuːədʃɪp ☆ 'stuːərd-] taking care of sb./sth.
39 **preserve sth.** [-'-] keep sth. in good condition
40 **be in line with sth.** be similar to sth.

1 Comprehension

a List the reasons given by Danaher why the global economy causes inequality.

b Fill in a copy of the table on 'globalization from below'.

Demands	Results for workers	Results for me
raise wages	higher pay	expensive goods
improve ...	...	...
...	...	...

c Make a similar table for 'globalization from above'.

2 Language work

a Match 1–9 with A–I to make expressions. Look at the text again if necessary.

1 remove	A unions
2 market	B elites
3 environmental	C wages
4 wealthy	D resources
5 trade	E barriers
6 moral	F pollution
7 human	G authority
8 raise	H needs
9 natural	I forces

b Complete the following sentences using five of the expressions from **a**.

1 The developed countries need the developing countries as most of the world's ..., such as iron, gas and minerals, can be found there.
2 Many countries want other countries to ... to trade, but are not so keen on doing so themselves.
3 The industrialized countries want ... to determine how the world economy works.
4 In developing countries there is often ..., as there are few laws regulating what emissions are allowed from factories.
5 Many international corporations do not want their workers to form ..., as they fear this could lead to strikes and higher wages.

3 Discussion

From what you have learned so far about globalization, discuss in class whether it brings with it more advantages or disadvantages.

4 Comment

Write a short comment (up to 300 words) on your attitude towards protest. Answering the following tasks/questions about the photos on the right may help you to gather your thoughts:

- Describe the different forms of protest.
- Which do you think are or aren't effective? Why (not)?
- In your opinion, are all forms of protest legitimate under certain circumstances?
- What issues might cause you to protest and how?

Creative protest

Violent protest

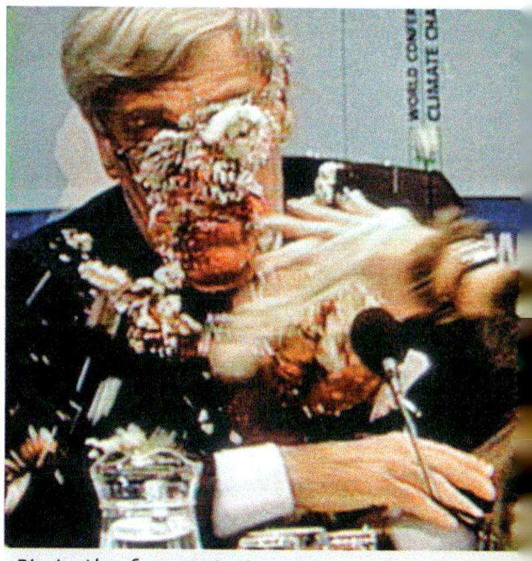
Pie-in-the-face protest

► Skill 3: Structuring a text (p. 34)

Webcode: TOP328857-19

largest • north • ratio • richest • size • smaller • south • wealth

Language help

- Comparing the two maps, you can see that ...
- There seems / doesn't seem to be a relationship between ... and ...
- The more/less populous a country, the ... it is.
- An exception to this is ...

5 Interpreting maps

a Complete the following sentences from a paragraph about the first map below. Use words from the box on the left.

1 In the map, the countries' ... depends not on geography, but on their ... .
2 As a result, the countries in the ... appear much larger than they really are.
3 The ones in the ... are considerably ... .
4 The United States is obviously the ... country, as it is by far the ... .
5 Western Europe is also quite big, but the ... of geographic size to wealth appears to be greatest for Japan, shown in purple.

b Write a similar paragraph describing the second map.

c Relate the two maps. It may help to look again at p. 18, ll. 9–19.
■ **Language help**

► Further Practice 9–10 (pp. 29–31)

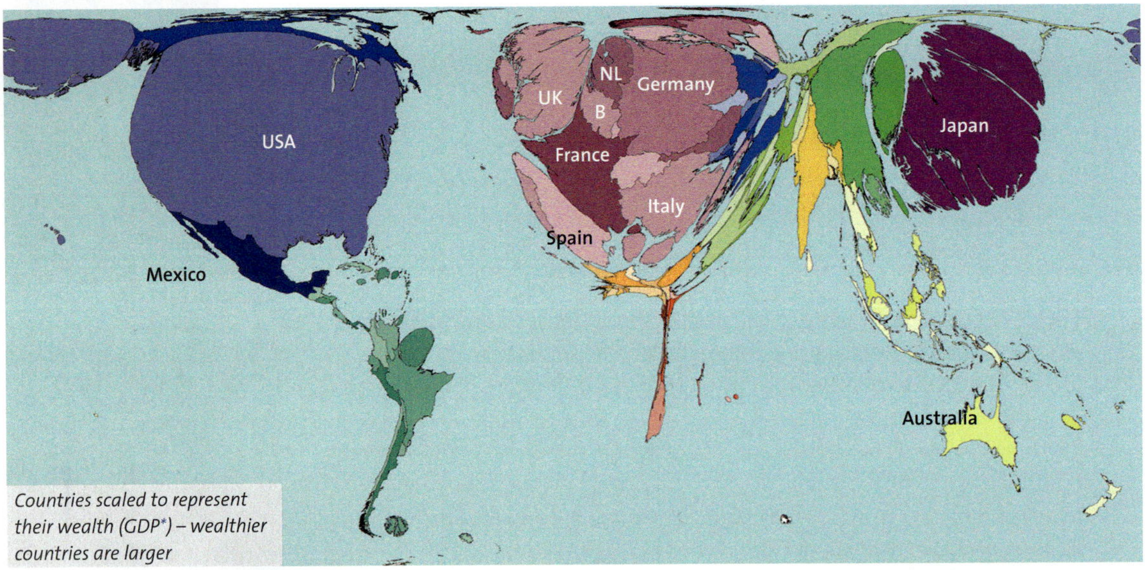

Countries scaled to represent their wealth (GDP) – wealthier countries are larger*

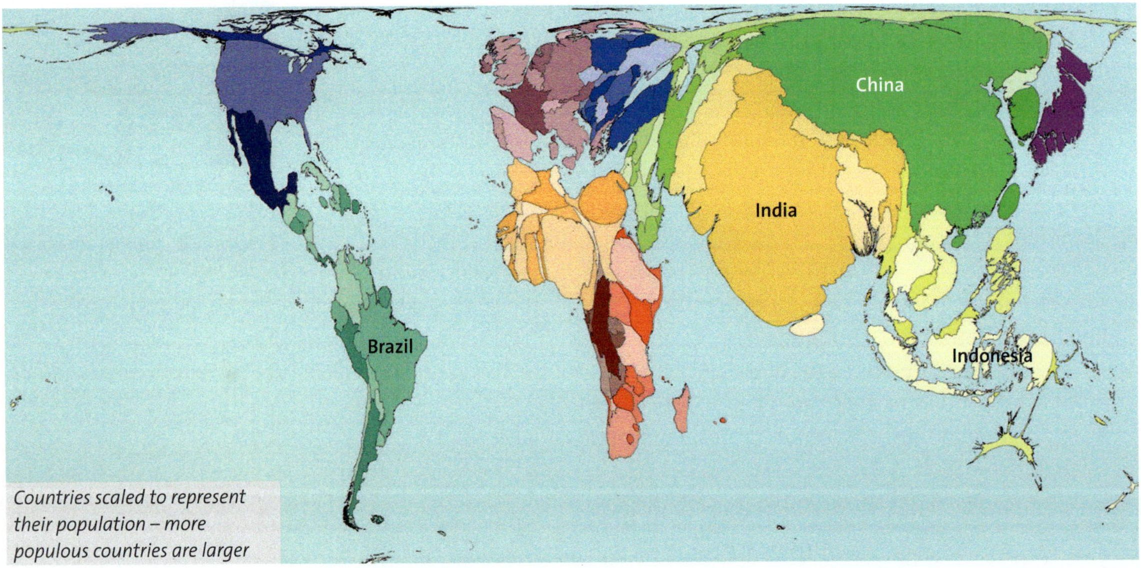

Countries scaled to represent their population – more populous countries are larger

Global Ties

C1 Towards Peace

A

B

C

D

1 A group puzzle

a Form four groups. Each group studies one of the photos above – A, B, C or D. Discuss what you know and what you think about the photo. Then read the headlines and match one to your photo, explaining why you think it fits.

1 'UNITING THE COMMONWEALTH* THROUGH SPORT'
2 'UN PEACEKEEPING* FORCE ARRIVES'
3 'EU* SWELLS TO 27 MEMBER STATES'
4 'DOCTORS WITHOUT BORDERS* TO THE RESCUE!'

b Each group member does further research on their photo and makes notes on how it relates to the title of this book and of Part C.

c Discuss your conclusions with your group. ▪ **Language help**

d Form new expert groups of four, where each person has studied a different photo. Ask each other about the different photos.

e Return to your group. Discuss and draw conclusions on how each of the photos could be seen as a step towards peace.

Language help

- the UN/EU/Commonwealth helps to ... by ...
- Voluntary organizations like ... can help with ..., but can't ...
- The conflict in ... has shown that ...
- Economic stability / personal contacts ... are vital / help to ...
- UN peacekeeping forces can only intervene when ...

C2 CD 02–03 A Model Power? David Miliband*

On 27 November 2007, the then British Foreign and Commonwealth Secretary David Miliband gave the opening address at the inauguration of the College of Europe, Bruges* [bruːʒ]. *The College chose that year to honour the memory of Anna Politkovskaya*, a regime-critical journalist murdered in Moscow in 2006, and Hrant Dink*, an Armenian-Turkish regime-critical journalist murdered in Istanbul earlier in the year.*

► Word Help (p. 43)

1 Listening for gist (first hearing)

a Note down which two of the following topics Miliband discusses in detail:

1 History 2 The single market 3 Threats to Europe today
4 Economics and protectionism 5 The EU as a model for the future

2 Listening for detail (second hearing)

a Point out Miliband's reasons for feeling personally committed to Europe.

b List the ways in which Miliband thinks the EU can be a model power.

3 After listening

a State in one or two sentences the speaker's attitude to the EU.

b Compare the content of the speech to the conclusions you reached in **C1**.

C3 60 Years of the Commonwealth* Paul Reynolds

In an article for the BBC Reynolds celebrates the sixtieth anniversary of the Commonwealth, Great Britain's special contribution to global stability.*

- Before reading the article, look at the world map at the back of this book. Identify on it as many countries of the Commonwealth as you can.

It is quite an achievement for the Commonwealth to have survived to the age of 60. It has been through three phases. The first was an over-ambitious attempt to subtly continue the British Empire by other means.

The second saw it torn apart by divisions, often over white rule in southern Africa, and was also marked by coups and chaos in many member states.

It wasn't until the third phase that it emerged into what it is today – a middle-ranking, reasonably useful organisation with a formal commitment to democracy and good governance and able to bring an influence to bear on regional problems within its orbit.

This is its perhaps suitably modest mission statement: "Fifty-three independent states consulting and co-operating in the common interests of their peoples and in the promotion of international understanding." [...]

The Millbrook Agreement in New Zealand in 1995 allows the Commonwealth to intervene diplomatically if democracy in a member state is undermined or abandoned, with the sanction of suspension from Commonwealth meetings.

A group of foreign ministers was set up to monitor the actions of member states. This shift enabled the Commonwealth to settle into a new role.

It even gained new members from outside the old empire. Portuguese-speaking Mozambique, attracted by the way in which the Commonwealth had acted against South Africa, joined in 1995. Partly French-speaking Cameroon also joined in 1995.

1 **achievement** success
2 **subtle** [ˈsʌtl] not noticeable or obvious
6 **middle-ranking** moderately important
8 **bring influence to bear on sth.** Einfluss auf etwas ausüben
9 **within its orbit** in its sphere of influence
10 **mission statement** declaration of aims
14 **undermine sth.** etwas untergraben
15 **abandon sth.** give sth. up altogether; **sanction of suspension** [ˈsæŋkʃn; səˈspenʃn] punishment of not being allowed to take part in sth.
19 **attract sb.** jdn. anziehen

And former members keep on coming back. South Africa rejoined in 1994, with warm words for the Commonwealth from Nelson Mandela, which did wonders for the organisation.

Pakistan, which left in 1972, came back in 1989 (though it has been suspended twice since then). Nigeria was suspended after executing an activist in 1995, but also returned, in 1999. [...]

Membership has always been valuable for the very smallest countries, of which there are many, some of them island states. They feel they have a voice in the world.

No Commonwealth conference goes by without the Maldives warning that its very future would be threatened by a rise in sea levels.

From: 'Life at 60 for the Commonwealth', website of the BBC, 9 March 2009

1 Comprehension

a State in your own words the three phases the Commonwealth has been through.

b Describe how the Commonwealth gives a voice to poor countries.

2 Beyond the text

a Do research to find out more about the particular events mentioned in the text. Then explain how the Commonwealth helps to encourage global peace and democracy.

b EXTRA Explain which of these expressions best describes the Commonwealth:

1 the British Empire in a new form
2 a community of English-speaking countries
3 an alternative United Nations*

TOPIC TASK

Write an essay called 'Peace and Stability in a Globalized World'.

a First brainstorm ideas that you have encountered in this book. Think about: financial aid, peaceful economic and political pressure, improving living standards, international organizations, peacekeeping forces, international contacts and friendships.

b Write an outline. Then write your essay.

▶ Skill 4: Writing an essay (p. 35)

Negotiation and Compromise

In order to achieve solutions which you desire, whether in private situations, at work or even in international negotiations, it is not enough just to believe that your views are correct or that your arguments will necessarily convince others. Sometimes you need to give a little in order to get what you want. That's easy if you follow a few simple rules:

1 *Make clear suggestions about what you want and have facts ready to support your arguments.*
2 *Be prepared to compromise.*
3 *Don't just reject the other person's ideas – make suggestions of your own. Stay polite – don't raise your voice, point or interrupt.*

1 CD 04 **Analysing a conversation**

Listen to the conversation. State where you think the man and the woman have followed the rules given above and where they haven't. Listen again and illustrate your answer with examples from the dialogue.

2 Mediation

a When mediating, it's often helpful to use introductory verbs to describe precisely what the different people are saying: are they asking for something, offering something or making a claim? Use appropriate introductory verbs from the box on the left and mediate the following statements.

admit that ...
agree to ...
claim that ...
demand that ...
offer to ...
promise to ...
regret (not) ...ing ...
suggest that ...

1 Kunde im Kaufhaus: Die ganzen Elektronikartikel sind hier überteuert. Im Elektromarkt kosten sie 10 bis 15% weniger.
The man claims that ...
2 Radfahrerin nach Unfall: Ich wäre unter gewissen Umständen bereit, einen Teil der Kosten zu tragen.
3 Gast in einer Pension: Ja, es stimmt schon, dass ich den Spiegel kaputt gemacht habe, aber er war nicht richtig angebracht.
4 Mann nach Streit: Das war wirklich blöd von mir. Tut mir leid. Ich hätte das nicht sagen sollen.
5 WG-Bewohnerin: Wie wäre es damit? Ich hole jeden zweiten Tag die Brötchen und mache das Frühstück, damit du ausschlafen kannst. Und dafür überlässt du mir an den Tagen dein Fahrrad.
6 WG-Bewohner: OK, ich bin mit deinen Bedingungen einverstanden.

b CD 05 Now mediate for the girl in the tense situation between English and German holidaymakers on the CD.

3 The stages of negotiation

a Whether formal or informal, negotiations usually follow a certain structure. Put these steps in the most likely order:

- Somebody sums up what has been agreed.
- One side or the other agrees to accept a compromise suggestion.
- The other side says what they want.
- Suggestions are made for possible compromises.
- Somebody states what they want.
- Arguments are traded back and forth.

b Match each phrase to one of the steps of negotiation from **a**.

- Try to see things from our point of view.
- I'd like to outline our objectives.
- Perhaps we can find some middle ground here.
- Let's look at what we've agreed so far.
- That sounds reasonable.
- That won't work for us. We'd like ...
- I don't have any problems with that.
- If you could see your way to accepting this, we would be willing to ...
- There are two main areas we'd like to discuss.
- We'd be prepared to ... provided that you ...
- So, if I see things correctly, we ...
- I'm afraid we can't accept that. We need to ...

4 Role-play: Negotiating in a model United Nations*

a Divide the class into nine groups. Each group will represent a country at the United Nations. (You will also need one person to act as Secretary General and run the meeting.) The countries are:

- developed countries: United Kingdom, United States of America, Germany
- newly industrialized countries: China, India, Mexico
- developing countries: Cambodia, Malawi, Peru

b Find out about the country your group will represent. Especially important are economic issues such as labour force and earnings, major industries, imports and exports.
Discuss in your group how your country should react to the following proposal for a UN resolution: 'All member countries commit to a minimum wage of US $1.50 per hour.' You can choose from the following arguments but should also try and come up with your own. Remember that you will not be representing your personal opinion, but that of your group's country. (Your globalization mind map will help you.)

Some arguments for a minimum wage:
- could raise the standard of living in developing countries
- would help prevent unfair competition between developing nations
- would help consumers who now have to worry about doing the right thing

Some arguments against a minimum wage:
- would be meaningless in countries that already pay higher wages
- might take away the competitive advantage that poorer countries now have for getting manufacturing jobs

'MAYBE YOU SHOULD RECONSIDER THOSE PLACE CARDS, MS. HARRIS?'

c Debate the proposition in the General Assembly. The Secretary General is in charge: 'I call this session of the General Assembly to order. We are here to debate the proposition that "All member countries ..."'
Each country has one ambassador, who will speak for the country – the other members advise him or her.

Words in Context
Everything Is Connected

1 Globalization puzzle ▸ Words in Context, pp. 8–9
Look at the clues below and find the missing words or phrases.

1 someone who uses the products made by industry (*c...*)
2 a person or company that provides people with work (*e...*)
3 a place where people work for very little money and have no job security (*s...*)
4 When jobs are moved to another country, they are *o...* .
5 '*P...* costs' means the amount of money it takes to make a product.
6 Globalization has become possible because of the *d...* of trade.
7 an organization that fights to protect the rights of people who work (*t... u...*)
8 all the people that are able to work in a country, city, etc. (*l... f...*)
9 a person who does a job that needs special training (*s... w...*)

Tip
Don't forget: no comma in defining relative clauses!

2 Paraphrasing ▸ Words in Context, pp. 8–9
Write your own definitions for the words below. Use relative clauses.

1 an employee
2 volunteer work
3 subsistence wage
4 donation
5 child labour

3 EXTRA Activate your vocabulary ▸ Words in Context, pp. 8–9
Translate the following sentences. The underlined expressions are from 'Words in Context'.

1 Die Arbeitskräfte in Ausbeuterbetrieben genießen keine Jobsicherheit.
2 Gewerkschaften kämpfen, um die Arbeitsbedingungen zu verbessern.
3 Die Firma hat die Produktionskosten gesenkt, indem sie einen Teil der Produktion nach Osteuropa *(Eastern Europe)* und Asien ausgegliedert hat.
4 Angebot und Nachfrage sind wichtige Faktoren in der Weltwirtschaft, aber viele Globalisierungskritiker machen sich Sorgen über die Auswirkungen der Konkurrenz auf die Entwicklungsländer.

Part A
Case Studies in Globalization

4 Interviewing a garment worker ▶ A2, pp. 11–12

What questions did the interviewer *(I)* ask Brinda *(B)*?

1 *I:* ...
B: My name's Brinda and I'm from Kodaikanal, north-west of Madurai, here in Tamil Nadu.
2 *I:* ...
B: Making jeans here? For about eight months now.
3 *I:* ...
B: Eleven hours a day. I start at 7 am and finish at 6 pm, when it gets dark.
4 *I:* ...
B: There was no work in my village, and my family need the money.
5 *I:* ...
B: I left school when I was 12.
6 *I:* ...
B: I send home nine hundred rupees* a month. That's half my wages.
7 *I:* ...
B: The last time? I saw my parents in December, when I had two days' holiday.
8 *I:* ...
B: Homesick? Yes, all the time. I miss my little brother and my 10-year-old sister.

* about 15 euros

5 If ... ▶ A2, pp. 11–12

a Complete the sentences below, using phrases from the box. Put the verbs in the correct tense.

be monitored more closely • *be too exhausted to cook* • *burst* • *have a guilty conscience* • *say that sweatshops are not really that bad* • *treat them to lunch* • *turn down my offer of food*

1 If I get a chance to interview these garment workers, I ...
2 I'll have to think of some other way of thanking them if they ...
3 If they had given me any more food, I think I ...
4 If I had to work such long hours, I ...
5 I would tell people in the USA about the conditions here if anyone ...
6 Working conditions would improve if the garment industry ...
7 If I paid the workers such low wages, I ...

Tip
The *if*-clause can come **after** the main clause. In this case we do not usually use a comma.

b Think about where your clothes are made and complete these sentences with your own ideas.

1 If I (don't) buy ... 2 If I worked ... 3 If I had known ...

Part B
The Globalized Economy

Language help
- **pay a bill/fine**, etc.
- **pay sb.** some money
- **pay for** goods/work/services, etc.

[1] **current account** Girokonto

6 Money matters ▸ B1, pp. 14–15

a Complete this conversation between a bank clerk and a new customer with words connected with money. They are all from **B1**.

New customer: I'd like to open an *a...* [1], please.
Bank clerk: What kind would that be, a *s...* [2] or a current account[1]?
New customer: Er, both, actually. I need to save money regularly, but I've just started work and my employers also have to transfer my wages to a bank. I also need easy access to my money.
Bank clerk: That's no problem. Whenever you need cash, you can make *w...* [3] at the counter or from the cash machine. And making *d...* [4] is just as easy when you want to pay money in. If you need to pay bills, our *o... b...* [5] service is very handy, because you can pay them by computer. If you want to exchange pounds into foreign *c...* [6] – into dollars or euros, for example – our rates are very good. We also offer easy credit to our *c...* [7] if they have a regular income and join our savings scheme. If at a later stage you wish to take out a *m...* [8] to buy a house, our rates are better than those of most other banks.

b CD 06 Listen to the complete dialogue and check your answers.

c Which English expressions from **6a** match these German expressions?

1 Bargeld brauchen
2 Geld abheben
3 Geld einzahlen
4 Geld sparen
5 Geld überweisen
6 eine Hypothek aufnehmen
7 ein Konto eröffnen
8 Rechnungen bezahlen

7 Everyday situations ▸ B2, pp. 16–17

What would you say in the following situations? Use modal verbs or their substitutes.

1 You're in a car with Dave. He's busy talking and doesn't notice that he's turning into a street with a 'No Entry' sign – it's a one-way street.
2 Your Scottish friends want you to go swimming with them. Tell them that you probably won't come along because the weather forecast says there's a possibility of a thunderstorm.
3 You recently saw a fantastic SF film, *The Day the Aliens Came*. Tell your friend Angus that it's absolutely vital that he sees it.
4 Your Irish host family want to visit you in Germany, but they're not keen on changing planes in London. Tell them it's not necessary to change – there are non-stop flights from Dublin.
5 A Welsh friend of yours is going on holiday to Sri Lanka. Tell her it's advisable to take anti-malaria tablets with her.
6 You're going to a shop in Dover to buy some sticky tape. Ask your host parents if they want you to get them a newspaper.
7 You're phoning your US friend Jo to say that you managed to get a cheap flight yesterday for 25th July, so you'll be able to visit her in Denver after all.

8 Countries ▸ B2, pp. 16–17

a Copy and complete the table. Look up any words you do not know.

Country	Adjective	Inhabitants
Trinidad	Trinidadian	Trinidadians
? ? ? ? ? ? ? ?	Belgian	? ? ? ? ? ? ? ?
? ? ? ? ? ? ? ?	Brazilian	? ? ? ? ? ? ? ?
Czech Republic	? ? ? ? ? ? ? ?	? ? ? ? ? ? ? ?
Denmark	? ? ? ? ? ? ? ?	? ? ? ? ? ? ? ?
? ? ? ? ? ? ? ?	? ? ? ? ? ? ? ?	French people
? ? ? ? ? ? ? ?	Irish	? ? ? ? ? ? ? ?
Malaysia	? ? ? ? ? ? ? ?	? ? ? ? ? ? ? ?
? ? ? ? ? ? ? ?	Pakistani	? ? ? ? ? ? ? ?
? ? ? ? ? ? ? ?	? ? ? ? ? ? ? ?	Poles
Switzerland	? ? ? ? ? ? ? ?	? ? ? ? ? ? ? ?
Taiwan	? ? ? ? ? ? ? ?	? ? ? ? ? ? ? ?

Tip 1
Don't look up each word separately: most dictionaries have lists of 'geographical names'. You can also look up 'nationality words' on the Internet.

Tip 2
The plural expressions *the Dutch*, *the English*, *the French*, *the Irish*, *the Swiss* and *the Welsh* are used for the **population** as a whole ('die Holländer', 'die Engländer', etc.).
To refer to the **inhabitants** (or groups of inhabitants), you have to use *Dutch*, *English*, *French*, *Irish*, *Swiss* and *Welsh* as adjectives followed by a suitable noun: (*two/many/several*) *Dutch* ***people***, *English* ***teenagers***, *French* ***musicians***, ...

Tip 3
Always use capital letters in English for countries, nationalities and languages.

b Choose one of these countries, find it on the map at the back of the book and say why you would/wouldn't like to visit it. Write about 60 to 90 words. Use all three of the words in the table for the country you have chosen.

9 Using the possessive form ▸ B3, pp. 18–20

a Use the *'s*- or *s'*-genitive as an alternative to the following phrases:

1 organizations for women
2 associations of farmers
3 the focus of the dominant system on greed
4 the accountability of the World Bank*
5 accounts for online savers
6 the policy of the IMF*
7 debts of foreign banks
8 the environment of our grandchildren

Tip
The *of*-phrase is usually used for things instead of the possessive form (*'s/s'*), e.g. *the beginning of the film*.
However, for things that are closely connected to people, e.g. countries, cities, institutions, the possessive form can also be used: *the government's policy*.

b Replace the underlined words and phrases by the *'s*-genitive. Be careful with the word order.

At present, 20% of the population <u>of the world</u> [1] has 83% of <u>global</u> income [2], with the poorest 60% of the people <u>in the world</u> [3] receiving only 5.6%. The richest 20% of the <u>world</u> population [4] consumes over 60% of the resources <u>worldwide</u> [5] and is responsible for about 75% of the environmental pollution <u>in the world</u> [6].

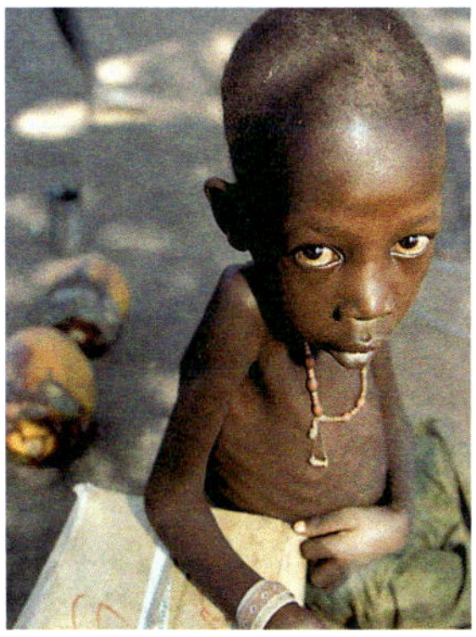

10 More globalization? ▸ B3, pp. 18–20

Paul Collier, the writer of the following article, is a Professor of Economics at the University of Oxford.

1 **staple** basic
3 **inconvenience** [ˌɪnkən'viːniəns] annoyance
6 **net buyer/**
8 **net purchaser** ['pɜːtʃəsə] sb. who buys more than they sell
10 **powder keg** Pulverfass
25 **replicate sth.** make an exact copy of sth.
26 **sophisticated** *(here)* well developed
27 **swath** [swɒθ ☆ swɑːθ] *(here)* area, region
33 **irredeemably** [ˌɪrɪ'diːməbli] unchangeably

The world price of staple foods has rocketed, almost doubling in the past 18 months. For consumers in the rich world this massive increase in the price of wheat or rice is an inconvenience; for consumers in the poorest countries it is a catastrophe.

Food accounts for around half of the entire budget of most Africans. Of course some poor households sell food, but many are net buyers. Indeed, decades of agricultural stagnation and growing populations have turned many African countries into food importers. The households that are poor and net purchasers of food are concentrated in the urban slums. These slums are already political powder kegs: rising food prices have triggered riots from Ivory Coast to Indonesia, from Burkina Faso to Bangladesh. Indeed they sow the seeds of an ugly and destructive populist politics.

Why have food prices rocketed? Paradoxically, this squeeze on the poorest has come about as a result of the success of globalisation in reducing world poverty. As China develops, helped by its massive exports to our markets, millions of Chinese households have started to eat better. Better means not just more food but more meat, the new luxury. But to produce 1kg of meat takes 6 kg of grain. Livestock reared for meat to be consumed in Asia are now eating the grain that would previously have been eaten by the African poor. So what is the remedy?

The best solution to a problem is often not to reverse what caused the problem. If you broke your leg by falling off a cliff, it is not a good idea to climb back up. The best solution to the rise in food prices is not to arrest globalisation. China's long march to prosperity is something to celebrate. The remedy to high food prices is to increase supply. The most realistic way is to replicate the Brazilian model of large, technologically sophisticated agro-companies that supply the world market. There are still many areas of the world – including large swaths of Africa – that have good land that could be used far more productively if it were properly managed by large companies. To contain the rise in food prices we need more globalisation, not less.

Brazil, the largest producer of sugarcane, is also the leading exporter of sugar.

Unfortunately, large-scale commercial agriculture is deeply, perhaps irredeemably, unromantic. We laud the production style of the peasant: environmentally sustainable and human in scale. In respect of manufacturing we grew out of this fantasy years ago, but in agriculture it continues to contaminate our policies. In Europe and Japan huge public resources have been devoted to propping up small farms. The best that can be said for these policies is that we can afford them.

In Africa, which cannot afford such policies, the World Bank and the Department for International Development have orientated their entire efforts on agricultural development to peasant-style production. Africa has less large-scale commercial agriculture than it had 60 years ago. Unfortunately, peasant farming is not well suited to innovation and investment. The result has been that African agriculture has fallen farther and farther behind.

Our longstanding agricultural romanticism has been compounded by our newfound environmental romanticism. In the United States fear of climate change has been manipulated by shrewd interests to produce grotesquely inefficient subsidies to biofuel. Around a third of American grain production has rapidly been diverted into energy production. This demonstrates both the superb responsiveness of the markets to price signals, and the shameful power of subsidy-hunting lobby groups. However, just as livestock are eating the food that would have been consumed by poor Africans, so Americans are running their SUVs on it. One SUV tank of biofuel uses enough grain to feed an African family for a year.

In Europe deep-seated fears of science have been manipulated into a ban on both the production and import of genetically modified crops. This has obviously retarded productivity growth in European agriculture. Again the best that can be said of it is that we are rich enough to afford such folly. But as an unintended side-effect it has terrified African governments into banning GM lest their farmers be shut out of European markets. Africa definitely cannot afford this self-denial. It needs all the help it can possibly get from GM drought-resistant crops.

While the policies needed for the long term have been befuddled by romanticism, the short-term global response has been pure beggar-thy-neighbour. It is easier for urban slum dwellers to riot than for farmers: riots need streets, not fields. And so, in the internal tussles between poor consumers and poor producers, the interests of consumers have prevailed in the developing countries.

Governments in grain-exporting countries, such as Argentina, have swung prices in favour of their consumers and against their farmers by banning or restricting exports. But such tariffs and export bans make investing in commercial-scale food production less attractive, drive up prices further still in the food-importing countries, and discourage farmers from increasing their yields, exacerbating global food shortages.

Unfortunately, trade in agricultural produce has been the main economic activity to have resisted the force of globalisation. The cost of this is now being picked up by the poorest people in the world.

From: Paul Collier, 'Food Shortages: Think Big', *The Times*, 15 April 2008

47 **compounded** made stronger
50 **subsidy** ['sʌbsədi] Subvention
53 **lobby group** Interessenverband; Lobby
57 **genetically modified** gentechnisch verändert
59 **folly** stupidity
60 **lest** *(fml)* in case
63 **befuddled** confused
66 **tussle** conflict
73 **exacerbate sth.** [ɪg'zæsəbeɪt] *(fml)* make sth. worse
76 **pick up the cost of sth.** *(infml)* pay for sth.

a Summarize the text, explaining briefly the problem poor Africans face and the writer's suggestion as to how to overcome it.

b In small groups, discuss arguments for and against Collier's suggestion. Give reasons from the text and add your own ideas.

c What do you think? State your own opinion of Collier's proposal for overcoming the global food shortage.

Either:

d Discuss whether the claims made in the article about 'agricultural' and 'environmental romanticism' in the Western world are true for Germany. Write a comment.

► Skill 3: Structuring a text (p. 34)

Or:

e Write an essay about the benefits of globalization. Include your own thoughts as well as potential counter-arguments to your points.

► Skill 4: Writing an essay (p. 35)

▸ Skill 1 Working with charts and graphs

When researching a topic, you will frequently come across statistics which are presented using a chart or graph. Moreover, when giving a presentation, you may find it useful to present figures you have found in a chart or graph.

pie chart

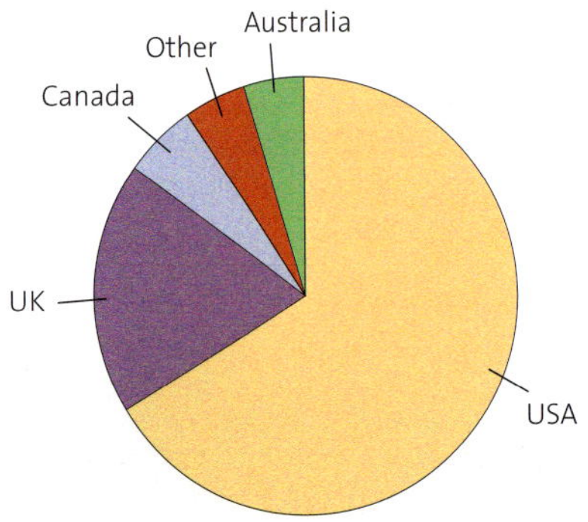

From: en.wikipedia.org

The pie chart[1] on the left shows the relative numbers of native English speakers in the major English-speaking countries of the world in 1997.

- A pie chart is divided into **slices**[2], or **sectors**, which represent parts of a whole – usually in the form of percentages of 100%. It can be an effective way of displaying information, particularly if you want to demonstrate the size of one slice as compared to the whole pie.
- The pie chart is said to be the most frequently used statistical chart in the business world and the media.

[1] **pie chart** Tortendiagramm, Kreisdiagramm [2] **slice** Anteil, Stück

bar chart

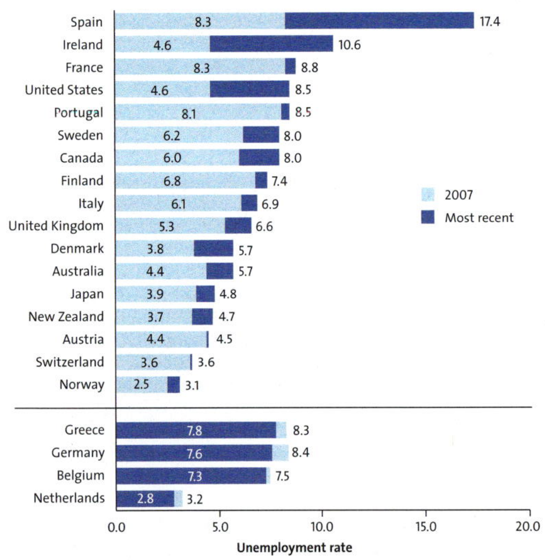

From: www.visualizingeconomics.com

The bar chart[3] on the left shows global unemployment rates and how they have developed.

- A bar chart is a chart with **rectangular**[4] **bars**, which can be either **horizontal** or **vertical**, whose lengths are proportional to the values they represent (here they are percentages).
- Bar charts are frequently used to compare two or more items, and they may also demonstrate changes over time, etc.

[3] **bar chart** Säulendiagramm, Balkendiagramm
[4] **rectangular** [rek'tæŋgjələ] rechteckig

line graph

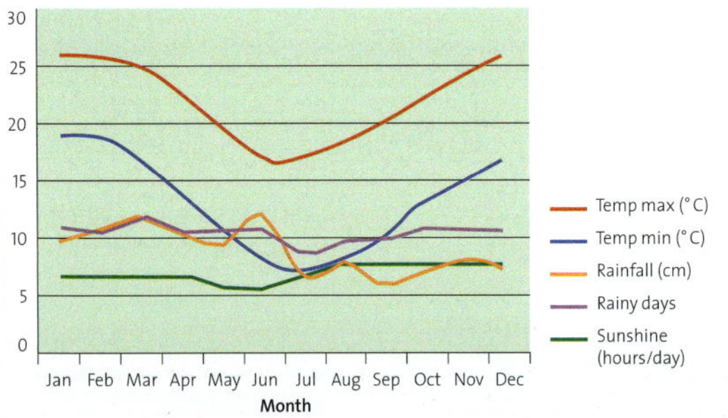

From: www.aussieworld.com

The line graph[5] on the left shows the weather conditions in Sydney, New South Wales (Australia).

- A line graph shows the relationship between numbers or items on the **vertical axis**[6] and on the **horizontal axis**. The measurements are **plotted**[7] or **charted**[8] between these two axes.
- A line graph is suitable for presenting continuity and trends.

[5] **line graph** Liniendiagramm [6] **axis** Achse, Koordinate
[7] **plot sth.** etwas einzeichnen, etwas eintragen [8] **chart sth.** etwas aufzeichnen, etwas darstellen

▸ Skill 2 Taking part in a discussion

*A discussion is a good way of exchanging ideas and forming an opinion. Most discussions are held spontaneously and in an informal manner, but in some cases it may be useful or necessary to elect a chairperson and hold an organized discussion (**Steps 1** and **4**). **Step 3** applies to both spontaneous and organized discussions.*

Step 1 (optional): Electing a chairperson
If you want to make sure the discussion is conducted in a disciplined manner, you can elect a chairperson to open and moderate the discussion and to keep track of whose turn it is.

Step 2: Preparing the discussion
- Collect ideas and information. You can do this alone or in a small group.
- Form an opinion on the topic or issue you are dealing with. Think of arguments for the opposing view and of ways to answer them. Make notes.

Step 3: Taking part in the discussion
Listen carefully to what other people say. Begin your contribution with an appropriate phrase:
- If you want to participate, wait until it's your turn, i.e. until the person speaking has finished. If you need to interrupt, do so politely.
  May I interrupt? / Excuse me, I would like to add to that. / That illustrates perfectly what I would like to say. ...
- If you want to back up what someone else has said, don't just repeat it, but add your own thoughts:
  Here's a good example of what I mean / what ... has just said. / Looking at the facts/figures, it's clear that ... / That statement is true/right/correct because ... / This proves what ... was saying ...
- Expressing agreement:
  I think ... is absolutely right when he/she says ... / I agree with ... because ...
- Respect what others are saying, even if you disagree:
  I take your point, but ... / I disagree / don't agree with ... / Did you really mean to say that ... ? / I see what you mean, but I don't believe/think that ... / I can't see why ...
- Asking for clarification:
  I'm sorry, but I don't understand/know what you mean by ... / Could you give an example / explain that, please? / Could you prove what you are saying? / If I understood you correctly ...
- Adding a point:
  Another thing is ... / What's more, ... / On top of that, ... / We must also consider ... / I would like to add to that ... / May I add ... ?

Step 4 (optional): Closing the discussion
The chairperson summarizes the arguments:
We have seen/heard that ... / The majority thinks that ... / Some are in favour of ..., others against ..., but in general you can say that ... / The general trend seems to be ... / On the one hand, ... on the other hand, ... / To sum up, ...

▶ Skill 3 Structuring a text

A well-structured text is easier to read and understand. The structure you use will depend on the kind of text you are writing. For instance, if you are telling a story or writing a report ▶ Skill 5*, you might want to relate events in chronological order. If you are writing an essay or discussing an issue, you should take an argumentative approach* ▶ Skill 4*. If you are writing a review, you should deal with one aspect of the novel or film at a time. However, there are some rules which apply to all kinds of texts:*

- Begin with an introduction, which can consist of one or more paragraphs. It should rouse the reader's interest and state clearly what the text is about. Here are some examples from different kinds of texts:
  Yesterday, Bristol Road was the scene of a terrible accident in which ...
  In the following essay, I will be dealing with the problem of ...
  I would like to present arguments in favour of ... and against ...
  ... is a fantastic novel/film which everyone should read/see ...
- In the main body, develop your ideas or present the events in the way you have decided on. Make your text coherent by using linking words.
  A witness reported that ...
  An example of the problem is that ...
  First of all, it is important that ... / Another important point to consider is ...
  The novel/film tells the story of Janet, a girl from ...
- In the conclusion, sum up what you have said and – if you are asked to – give your own opinion.
  Considering the damage to the cars involved, the victims were lucky that ...
  My own view of the matter/problem is that ...
  All in all, it can be said that ...
  The novel/film has something for everyone ...

In addition, there are other elements that help to structure a text making it easier to read and understand:

- Begin a new paragraph for each new event, point, argument or idea.
- Use topic sentences in your paragraphs: The first sentence states the theme. The following sentences give supporting material by citing concrete examples. The last sentence in a paragraph draws a general conclusion from the given examples.
- Structure your text visually, for example by leaving spaces between your paragraphs.

▶ Skill 4 Writing an essay

When writing an essay you are required to present a topic in a coherent way, for example by presenting arguments for and against a topic.

Step 1: Read the task carefully and pay particular attention to the special vocabulary used in tasks, so that you know exactly what is required of you.
Step 2: Proceed as you would with any other text, from first draft to final draft giving yourself enough time to re-read your essay and check for grammar and spelling mistakes, but consider the following points as well:

- In your introduction restate the problem from your task. You can also state your main points and explain the structure of your text ▶ **Skill 3**.
- Present your arguments in the main part of your essay. Devote one paragraph to each of the arguments. Use connectors to make your text coherent ▶ **Skill 3**.
- If you are asked to analyse or examine an issue, arrange your arguments according to their importance, from the weakest to the strongest point or vice versa.
- If you are asked to discuss a topic, i.e. weigh up the pros and cons, you can take the argumentative approach and deal with all the arguments in favour of the topic first and then all the arguments against the topic next. Alternatively, you can discuss one aspect at a time, presenting ideas for and against each aspect one after the other.
- If you are asked to compare two things, deal with the similarities first and then the differences or vice versa.
- Make a concluding statement in which you sum up your arguments ▶ **Skill 3**.

'And this student model is programmed with the answers to 500 popular essay questions.'

▶ Skill 5 Writing a report

Reports aim at providing factual information about an event in an objective manner and in a way that can be easily understood by the reader.

There are a few points which you should bear in mind when writing a report:

- Prepare your information carefully.
- Present your information in a direct way. It should be accurate as well as clear and easily understood by the reader.
- Concentrate on the facts giving answers to the questions *Who? What? When? Where? Why?* and *How?*
- Give the most important information first and provide details afterwards.
- Use formal language. Your report should be objective in style as well as content. Avoid mentioning your own personal feelings and thoughts, although you might be asked to state your own opinion at the end.
- Use pictures, diagrams or charts to illustrate your report and to make it clearer and easier to understand.
- Use quotes.

Vocabulary you should learn (from pages 6–23)

p. 6

Lead-in

How come?	'Mom is angry at me.' – **'~ come?'** – 'I forgot Mother's Day.'	*Warum? Wie kommt das?*
(to) **hijack** sth. ['haɪdʒæk]	The terrorists **~ed** a plane that was supposed to fly to New York.	*etwas entführen*
natural resources *(pl)* [ˌnætʃrəl rɪ'sɔːsɪz, rɪ'zɔːsɪz ☆ 'riːsɔːrsɪz]	Despite being rich in **~ resources**, some African countries have high rates of poverty.	*Bodenschätze; Rohstoffquellen*

p. 8

Words in Context: Everything Is Connected

globalization [ˌgləʊbəlaɪ'zeɪʃn]	*word family:* globe – global – (to) globalize – **globalization**	*Globalisierung*
breaking down of trade barriers ['bæriəz]	The **~ down of trade ~** has made international trade easier.	*Abbau von Handelsgrenzen*
supporters of globalization [sə'pɔːtəz]	The **~ of globalization** see the trend as an opportunity to improve intercultural relations.	*Globalisierungs-befürworter/innen*
deregulation [ˌdiːregju'leɪʃn]	= (market) opening	*Deregulierung; Marktöffnung*
developing country [dɪ'veləpɪŋ]	*other collocations with* **developing***:* ~ area / economy / nation / system	*Entwicklungsland*
access to world markets ['ækses]	*other collocations with* **access to***:* **~ to** employment / good resources / the Internet	*Zugang zu Weltmärkten*
competition [ˌkɒmpə'tɪʃn]	*word family:* (to) compete with/against sb. – **competition** – competitive – competitor	*Wettbewerb*
consumer [kən'sjuːmə]	Nowadays many food **~s** favour organic food.	*Konsument/in, Verbraucher/in*
developed country [dɪ'veləpt]	= industrialized country	*Industrieland*
market forces	**Market ~** have driven up the price of oil.	*Marktkräfte*
supply and demand [sə'plaɪ, dɪ'mɑːnd]	A change in the **supply and ~** will have an effect on the price – either for better or for worse!	*Angebot und Nachfrage*
globalization critic ['krɪtɪk]	Many **globalization ~s** lament the loss of national identity through globalization.	*Globalisierungskritiker/in*

(p.8)	**unsafe and unhealthy condition** [ʌn,helθi kən'dɪʃn]	*other collocations with* **condition**: chronic / critical / general / original ~	*unsicherer und ungesunder Zustand*
	sweatshop ['swetʃɒp]	= a place where people work for low wages in poor conditions	*Ausbeuterbetrieb*
	earn a subsistence wage [ɜ:n, səb'sɪstəns]	Workers in developing countries often **earn a subsistence ~**.	*einen Lohn verdienen, der nur den Lebensunterhalt deckt*
	(to) **enjoy job security** [sɪ'kjʊərəti]	*other collocations with* **enjoy**: (to) ~ a good view / a meal / a privilege / good health / life	*Jobsicherheit genießen*
	child labour ['leɪbə]	Unfortunately, many companies in the fashion industry rely on **child ~**.	*Kinderarbeit*
	trade union [,treɪd 'ju:niən]	**T~ unions** fight for the rights of workers and employees.	*Gewerkschaft*
	(to) **organize workers** ['ɔ:gənaɪz]	*other collocations with* **organize**: (to) ~ a festival / an excursion / a world tour / one's time	*Arbeiter organisieren*
	(to) **improve working conditions** [ɪm'pru:v]	*other collocations with* (to) **improve**: (to) ~ performance / standards / efficiency	*Arbeitsbedingungen verbessern*
	skilled worker	'**S~ workers** from abroad are highly welcome in our country,' he said.	*gelernte Arbeitskraft; Fachkraft*
	unskilled worker	Finding a well-paid job is difficult for him, since he is an **~ worker**.	*ungelernte Arbeitskraft; Hilfsarbeiter/in*
	employer [ɪm'plɔɪə]	*word family*: (to) employ – employ *(n)* – employable – employee – **employer** – employment	*Arbeitgeber/in*
	production cost [prə'dʌkʃn kɒst]	**Production ~s** have risen in line with the price of oil.	*Produktionskosten*
	plant [plɑ:nt]	Multinational companies have different **~s** all over the world.	*Niederlassung; Werksanlage*
	domestic production [də'mestɪk]	*other collocations with* **domestic**: ~ affaires / flights / politics / violence	*Inlandsproduktion*
	(to) **outsource** sth. ['aʊtsɔ:s]	By **~sourcing** marketing, the company became more efficient and saved millions of dollars.	*etwas ausgliedern; etwas nach außen verlagern*
	labour force	= all the people available to work (in a company, city or country)	*Arbeitskraft*
	employee [ɪm'plɔɪi:]	= sb. who is employed in a firm, factory or company	*Angestellte/r, Mitarbeiter/in*

(p.8)	**wage**	*synonyms:* earnings *(pl)* / pay / salary	*Gehalt*
	boycott *(n)* ['bɔɪkɒt]	By organizing **~s**, employees can put pressure on their employers.	*Boykott; Verweigerung; Lahmlegung*
	multinational company [ˌmʌltiˌnæʃnəl 'kʌmpəni]	*other collocations with* **multinational***:* ~ corporation / force / organization / state	*multinationaler Konzern*
	brand	*synonyms:* label / make / type	*Marke*
	image ['ɪmɪdʒ]	The company spent millions on advertising last year to develop its ~ as a family brand.	*Image; Persönlichkeitsbild*
	bad press	**Bad** ~ can ruin a company's image forever.	*schlechte Presse*
	(to) **import goods** [ɪm'pɔːt]	*opposite:* (to) export goods	*Güter importieren*
	(to) **protect the rights of workers** [prə'tekt]	*other collocations with* **protect***:* (to) ~ consumers / a file / jobs	*die Rechte der Arbeiter/ -innen schützen*
	globalization opponent [ə'pəʊnənt]	Many **globalization ~s** see the trend as a threat to cultural traditions. = globalization critic	*Globalisierungsgegner/in*
	fair trade	*other collocations with* **trade***:* domestic / flourishing / foreign / free / international / overseas / slave ~	*fairer Handel*
	workplace	It is important to feel comfortable at your ~.	*Arbeitsplatz*
	global economy [ˌgləʊbl‿ɪ'kɒnəmi]	Nowadays we have a ~ **economy** where one economy is no longer independent from another.	*Weltwirtschaft*
	financial crisis [faɪˌnænʃl 'kraɪsɪz]	*other collocations with* **financial***:* ~ adviser / aid / difficulties / means / year	*Finanzkrise*
	(to) **bankrupt** sb./sth. ['bæŋkrʌpt]	He took a risk that could have **~ed** his company.	*jdn./etwas bankrott machen*
	government intervention [ˌɪntə'venʃn]	Changes in the economy led to **government** ~ and changes in financial laws.	*Eingriff der Regierung*
	international trade [ˌɪntə'næʃnəl]	*other collocations with* **international***:* ~ airport / company / school / law / relations	*internationaler Handel*
	(to) **regulate** sth. ['regjuleɪt]	*synonyms:* (to) determine sth. / (to) govern sth. / (to) influence sth. / (to) order sth.	*etwas regulieren*
	industrialized country [ɪn'dʌstriəlaɪzd]	= developed country	*Industrieland*
	international relations [rɪ'leɪʃnz]	*other collocations with* **relations***:* diplomatic / foreign / sexual ~	*internationale Beziehungen*

(p.8)

peacekeeping mission ['mɪʃn]	There was a heated debate about the ~ **mission** in Afghanistan.	*friedenserhaltende Mission*
relief effort [rɪ'li:f‿ˌefət]	A charity in Africa launched an international ~ **effort** to save lives.	*Hilfsmaßnahme*
government funding ['fʌndɪŋ]	The automobile industry benefited from **government** ~.	*staatliche Finanzierung*
donation [də'neɪʃn]	The church collected **~s** for children in Africa.	*Spende*
volunteer work [ˌvɒlən'tɪə]	More and more young people are choosing to do ~ **work** after graduation or during vacation.	*ehrenamtliche Arbeit*

Part A:
Case Studies in Globalization

p.10

A1 The Price Make-up of a €100 Sport Shoe

profit ['prɒfɪt]	*opposite:* loss	*Gewinn*
subcontractor [ˌsʌbkən'træktə ☆ sʌb'kɑ:ntræktər]	= a person or company that does part of the work given to another person or company	*Zulieferer/in; Subunternehmer/in*
retailer ['ri:teɪlə]	**R~s** are highly dependent on their clients' liquidity.	*Einzelhändler*
VAT = value added tax ['vælju:]	In German supermarkets prices include ~.	*Umsatzsteuer*
advertising ['ædvətaɪzɪŋ]	The biggest brands spend huge amounts of money on ~ to ensure their success.	*Werbung*

p.11

A2 The Jeans

freelance ['fri:lɑ:ns]	*opposite:* permanently employed	*freiberuflich*
(to) **treat sb. to** sth. [tri:t]	You won't believe it: My boss **~ed** us **to** lunch in a fancy restaurant today!	*jdn. zu etwas einladen*
(to) **uncover** sth. [ʌn'kʌvə]	*synonyms:* (to) reveal sth. / (to) unveil sth.	*etwas aufdecken, etwas enthüllen*
(to) **be subject to** sth. ['sʌbdʒekt]	The train times **are ~ to** change due to roadworks.	*einer Sache unterliegen*
(to) **market** sth. **as** sth. ['mɑ:kɪt]	The company chose to change the recipe and to ~ the drink **as** a health product.	*etwas als etwas verkaufen*

(p.11)	**conscience** ['kɒnʃəns]	I told my mum a lie and had a bad ~ for the rest of the day.	*Gewissen*

p.13

A3 Outsourcing

supervisor ['suːpəvaɪzə]	My ~ called me for a meeting and told me that he was unhappy with my work.	*Abteilungsleiter/in*

Part B:
The Globalized Economy

p.14

B1 Global Money, Global Crisis

municipality [mjuːˌnɪsɪ'pæləti]	Laws may be different, depending on the ~ you are in.	*Gemeinde, Kommune*
savings account [ə'kaʊnt]	When I was born, my parents opened a ~ **account** for my college education.	*Sparkonto*
withdrawal [wɪð'drɔːəl]	*opposite:* deposit *(n)*	*Kontoabhebung*
state ownership ['əʊnəʃɪp]	*other collocations with* **ownership***:* collective / joint / private / public ~	*Staatsbesitz*
asset ['æset]	As time passed, his **~s** grew – his savings gained interest, his stocks improved, and he even inherited more land.	*Anlage; Kapital; Vermögen*
tenfold	= multiplied by ten	*zehnfach*
mortgage ['mɔːgɪdʒ]	After Phil lost his job, they could not afford to pay the ~ and moved to a smaller house.	*Hypothek*
(to) **get around**	Keep this a secret – I don't want it to **get** ~.	*sich herumsprechen*
deposit [dɪ'pɒzɪt]	I was paid in cash so I went to the bank to make a ~.	*Einzahlung*
(to) **be in charge**	Just be quiet and listen to me! I **am in** ~ here!	*die Verantwortung tragen*

p.16

B2 The Butterfly Effect

fieldwork	Scientists journeyed through the jungle for days to conduct some ~ on a new species of spider.	*Feldforschung*
global interconnectedness [ˌɪntəkə'nektdnəs]	*other collocations with* **global***:* ~ market / player / village / warming	*globale Vernetzung*
cumulative effect [ˌkjuːmjələtɪv‿ɪ'fekt]	Global warming is the ~ **effect** of centuries of industry.	*kumulativer Effekt, geballter Effekt*

momentous [mə'mentəs ☆ moʊ'mentəs]	9/11 was a ~ occasion in American history and will never be forgotten.	*bedeutsam; folgenschwer*
outcome ['aʊtkʌm]	*synonyms:* consequence / effect / result	*Folge(n); Resultat*
(to) **relativize** sth. ['relətɪvaɪz]	Through his comparison he attempted to ~ the problem.	*etwas relativieren; etwas verkleinern*
(to) **exercise power over** sb.	*other collocations with* **exercise***:* (to) ~ care / control / discretion / patience	*Macht über jdn. ausüben*

p.18 **B3 Global Protest**

(to) **proceed** [prə'si:d ☆ proʊ'si:d]	*synonyms:* (to) continue / (to) carry on / (to) go on / (to) move on	*fortfahren, weitergehen*
(to) **pressure** sb. ['preʃə]	*word family:* (to) press sth. – pressure *(n)* – (to) **pressure** sb.	*Druck auf jdn. ausüben*
wealthy elite [ˌwelθɪ‿eɪ'li:t]	Not even the **wealthy ~s** are safe from the effects of the financial crisis.	*reiche Elite*
greed	**G~** for profit was one of the main reasons for the financial crisis.	*Geldgier; Habgier*
accountability [əˌkaʊntə'bɪləti]	The question of ~ came up again and again – who was to blame?	*Verantwortlichkeit*

Part C:
Global Ties

pp. 22-23 **C3 60 Years of the Commonwealth**

over-ambitious [ˌəʊvəræm'bɪʃəs]	The ~ girl would stop at nothing to get everything she wanted.	*übertrieben ehrgeizig*
reasonably *(adv)* ['ri:znəbli]	*synonym:* fairly	*relativ; einigermaßen*
(to) **be threatened by** sth. ['θretnd]	The survival of polar bears **is ~ by** the rise in sea levels.	*bedroht sein von*

More useful vocabulary to help you discuss the themes in this book

Trade and Finance

currency ['kʌrənsi]	*collocations with* **currency***:* single / foreign ~	*Währung*
economy [ɪ'kɒnəmi]	*word family:* (to) economize – **economy** – economist – economic	*Wirtschaft*
exchange rate [ɪks'tʃeɪndʒ]	the rate at which one currency can be converted into another	*Wechselkurs*
free trade [ˌ– '–]	trade between countries where there are no restrictions in place	*Freihandel*
international trade	*other collocations with* **trade***:* ethical / fair / slave ~	*internationaler Handel*
trade barriers ['bæriəz]	*other collocation with* **trade***:* ~ agreement	*Handelsschranke*

Living in a Globalized World

(to) **outsource** ['aʊtsɔːs]	*synonym:* (to) subcontract	*outsourcen, auslagern*
consumer [kən'sjuːmə]	*word family:* (to) consume – consumption – **consumer**	*Konsument/in, Verbraucher/in*
debt relief ['det rɪˌliːf]	the practice of letting poorer nations not pay back the money they owe to richer countries	*Schuldenerlass*
developed country	*opposite:* developing country	*Industrieland*
emerging market [ɪ'mɜːdʒɪŋ]	country which is undergoing a process of rapid industrial growth	*Schwellenland*
exploitation [ˌeksplɔɪ'teɪʃn]	*word family:* (to) exploit sth./sb. – **exploitation** – exploiter	*Ausbeutung*
living standard	*other collocation with* **living***:* ~ conditions	*Lebensstandard*
merger ['mɜːdʒə]	The ~ between the two companies last year was a success – they're making a profit now!	*Firmenzusammenschluss, Fusion*
multinational *(n)* [ˌmʌlti'næʃnəl]	The ~ has branches all over the world, but its headquarters are in Paris.	*multinationaler Konzern*
poverty ['pɒvəti]	*opposite:* wealth	*Armut*
sweatshop ['swetʃɒp]	Mira worked in a **~shop** in Delhi making clothes for international fashion labels.	*Ausbeuterbetrieb*

Selected vocabulary from the accompanying audios and videos to assist comprehension

p.13

A3 DVD Outsourcing

gratification *(fml)* [ˌgrætɪfɪ'keɪʃn]	satisfaction
(to) **haze**	(to) play tricks on sb. or give them unpleasant things to do
(to) **quit** *(infml)*	(to) leave your job or school
up to speed (**on** sth.)	(of a person, company, etc.) doing sth. at the expected rate or level
MPI = Minutes per Incident ['ɪnsɪdənt]	*(here)* Zeit zur Bewältigung eines Verkaufsgespräches
fair enough *(BE, infml)*	used to express that an idea seems practical
upset (about sth.**)/(that)** *(adj)*	unhappy, disappointed (about sth./that)
(to) **rig**	(to) influence or manipulate sth. in order to get the results you want
hard drive ['- -]	Festplatte

p.22

C2 CD 02–03 A Model Power?

treaty	formal agreement between two or more countries
posterity *(fml)* [pɒ'sterəti]	all the people who will live in the future
strife *(fml)*	conflict
(to) **convene** *(fml)* [kən'viːn]	(to) arrange for a group of people to come together for a formal meeting
(to) **engage in** sth.	(to) be involved in sth., take part in sth.
(to) **stave** sth. **off**	(to) delay sth.
(to) **peddle** sth.	(to) express an idea/tell a story to different people in order to make them accept it
scramble for sth.	fight, chase for sth.
rogue *(adj)* [rəʊg]	behaving in ways that are not expected or not normal, often in a destructive way
raison d'être *(French)* [ˌreɪzɒ̃ 'detrə]	most important reason for sb.'s/sth.'s existence
clout [klaʊt]	power and influence
(to) **chart**	(to) plan a course of action
(to) **dispense** sth. (**to** sb.) *(fml)* [dɪ'spens]	(to) provide sth. (for people)

TERMS

College of Europe
founded in 1949, an independent university institute which offers students a Master's degree programme in European Studies. The College has two campuses, one in Bruges, Belgium, and another in Natolin, Poland.

Commonwealth
an association of 54 nations from six continents. Member nations work together on issues of development, democracy, freedom and peace. They support each other and establish common rules and values on a democratic basis. Those values are monitored and protected by the Commonwealth Ministerial Action Group (CMAG), which is a rotating group of nine foreign ministers. CMAG may report to heads of government if a member should be suspended or expelled. The head of the Commonwealth is Queen Elizabeth II. She has symbolic functions such as giving speeches, holding discussions and visiting the host country of each Commonwealth's summit. Decisions are made between the heads of government or the ministers responsible for a particular department. Three intergovernmental institutions of the association – the Commonwealth Secretariat, the Commonwealth Foundation and the Commonwealth of Learning – help implement the association's plans and decisions.

Commonwealth Games
a multi-sports competition that takes place every four years. It involves the 54 member states of the Commonwealth and, in addition to many Olympic sports, it includes some that are only played in the Commonwealth countries, e.g. lawn bowls. The first games were held in Hamilton, Ontario, Canada, in 1930. In 2014 Glasgow, Scotland, will host the next event.

Doctors Without Borders
cf. Médecins Sans Frontières

European Union

both a political and economic union that counts 27 member states today. Due to EU laws that are binding for all member states money, people, services and goods may move freely within the Union. 17 member states also share the euro as a currency. The EU includes several important institutions such as the European Commission or the Court of Justice of the European Union. Every five years, EU citizens can elect members of the European Parliament directly.

GDP (= gross domestic product)
the economic term given to the total market value of goods and services produced by the economy of a country in a particular period of time. The GDP is often used to assess the economic health of a country.

Group of Eight (G8)

an important international forum made up of the eight economically most powerful countries (Canada, France, Germany, Italy, Japan, Russia, the UK and the USA). Founded in 1975 as the G6 (Canada joined a year later, Russia in 1998), the group has set itself the task of trying to solve world problems such as poverty. Its meetings, attended by the heads of the member countries as well as the head of the European Union, are often controversial.

International Monetary Fund (IMF)

an organization founded in 1944 to oversee the international finance system and stabilize exchange rates between different countries' currencies. Critics say its politics benefit richer nations, especially the USA.
The IMF has its headquarters in Washington, D.C.

Médecins Sans Frontières (Doctors Without Borders)

an international medical humanitarian organization working in more than 60 countries to assist people whose survival is threatened by violence, neglect or catastrophe. In 1999 *Médecins Sans Frontières* received the Nobel Peace Prize.

non-governmental organizations (NGOs)

private organizations that are officially recognized by governments, but are set up and managed independently of them and therefore function without government status. Although NGOs may be funded by the state, governments have no influence upon how they are run. They usually have a social aim, e.g. community development, provision of social services or environmental protection.

Outsourced

a romantic comedy film (directed by John Jeffcoat, released in 2006, screenplay by George Wing, John Jeffcoat) in which Todd (Josh Hamilton), supervisor of a Seattle sales call centre, is outsourced to India and travels to Mumbai to train his replacement. Facing the chaos in the streets of Mumbai and an office paralyzed by constant cultural misunderstandings, Todd yearns to go back as fast as possible. Before long, Todd finds himself disarmed by the friendliness of his likeable replacement Puro (Asif Basra) and charmed by co-worker Asha (Ayesha Dharker) who helps him to familiarize himself with the people and customs of India. Todd realizes that there's a lot to learn for him too and in the end discovers that being outsourced may be the best thing that ever happened to him.

Oxfam (Oxford Committee for Famine Relief)

founded in 1942 as Oxfam UK, Oxfam is an international confederation of 14 development NGOs working together and with partners and allies in 100 countries around the world to find lasting solutions to poverty and injustice.

United Nations (UN)

an international organization founded in 1945 by 51 countries intending international peace and security. Today the organization with its 192 member states works in a wide range of areas from environment and refugees' protection, disaster relief and economic and social development to promoting democracy and human rights for a safe world in the future.
Drafted immediately after the Second World War, the Charter of the United Nations set out to formulate the aims of this new organization:

> WE, THE PEOPLES OF THE UNITED NATIONS, DETERMINED,
> to save succeeding generations from the scourge[1] of war, which twice in our lifetime has brought untold sorrow to mankind, and
> to reaffirm[2] faith in fundamental human rights, in the dignity and worth of the human person, in the equal rights of men and women and of nations large and small, and
> to establish conditions under which justice and respect for the obligations[3] arising from treaties and other sources of international law can be maintained, and
> to promote social progress and better standards of life in larger freedom,
> AND FOR THESE ENDS[4]
> to practise tolerance and live together in peace with one another as good neighbours, and
> to unite our strength to maintain international peace and security, and
> to ensure[5], by the acceptance of principles and the institution of methods, that armed force shall not be used, save in the common interest, and
> to employ international machinery for the promotion of the economic and social advancement of all peoples,
> HAVE RESOLVED[6] TO COMBINE OUR EFFORTS TO ACCOMPLISH THIS AIM.

Preamble to the Charter of the United Nations (1945)

1 **scourge** [skɜːdʒ] *(fig)* person or thing that causes suffering
2 **reaffirm sth.** etwas erneut bekräftigen
3 **obligation** Verpflichtung
4 **end** aim, purpose
5 **ensure sth.** *(BE)* = *(AE)* insure sth., guarantee sth.
6 **resolve** [rɪˈzɒlv ☆ -ˈzɑːlv] decide firmly

UN peacekeeping mission

The first UN peacekeeping mission took place in 1948. UN military observers were sent to the Middle East to monitor the Armistice Agreement between Israel and its Arab neighbours. With its missions the UN seeks to help countries in times of conflict and war. So far, there have been a total of 64 UN peacekeeping operations around the world.

World Bank

a financial institution founded in 1945 to lend money to poorer countries so that they could develop their economies by building roads, schools, etc. Often this has worked, but sometimes loans have been stolen by corrupt politicians and many developing countries have been left with huge debts they cannot repay. The World Bank has its headquarters in Washington, D.C.

World Trade Organization (WTO)

WORLD TRADE ORGANIZATION

an international organization consisting of 153 members. It was set up in 1995 and controls and deals with global rules of trade between nations. In addition to the Ministerial Conference in Geneva, Switzerland, which makes the top decisions, there are also a number of working groups and committees like the Goods Council and the Services Council. The WTO has a dispute settlement role and may authorize retaliation ('Strafmaßnahmen') against countries who violate the rules.

PERSONS

Danaher, Dr Kevin

an expert on the green economy and globalization and a co-founder of the NGO Global Exchange (1988). Danaher is a frequent speaker at universities and community organizations as well as an author and editor of numerous books (e.g. *Building the Green Economy: Success Stories from the Grass Roots*, 2007).

Diana, Princess of Wales (1961–1997)

the wife of Prince Charles between 1981 and 1996, when they divorced. She was respected for her charity work, including support for an international ban on the use of landmines, and was one of the most photographed celebrities of the last century. She and her partner, Dodi Fayed, an Egyptian business tycoon, were killed in a car accident in Paris in 1997 while being followed by paparazzi.

Dink, Hrant (1954–2007)

a journalist, editor and columnist of Turkish-Armenian descent. He was a prominent member of the Armenian minority in Turkey, best known for advocating Turkish-Armenian reconciliation and human and minority rights in Turkey. Dink was assassinated in Istanbul in January 2007 by a 17-year old Turkish nationalist.

Eriksen, Thomas Hylland (born 1962)

a social anthropologist at the Department of Social Anthropology, University of Oslo, Norway. His professional work has largely focused on identity politics and globalization. He wrote essays and articles on numerous topics, academic and non-academic. From 1993 to 2001, he was editor of a general cultural journal covering politics, literature and culture.

Miliband, David Wright (born 1965 in London)

the son of immigrants to the UK. He was educated in London, graduated with First Class Honours in Philosophy, Politics and Economics from Corpus Christi College, Oxford University, and completed a Masters Degree in Political Science at the Massachusetts Institute of Technology, where he was a Kennedy Scholar. He is a British Labour politician and has been the Member of Parliament for South Shields since 2001. From June 2007 until May 2010 he was the Secretary of State for Foreign and Commonwealth Affairs.

Politkovskaya, Anna (1958–2006)

a Russian-American journalist well known for her coverage and opposition to the Chechen conflict. She received numerous awards for her work, among them the Amnesty International Global Award for Human Rights Journalism in 2001 and the Lettre Ulysses Award for the Art of Reportage in 2003. On 7 October 2006 she was assassinated in her apartment building in Moscow.

Timmerman, Kelsey (born 1975)

a freelance writer and journalist. He has a passion for travelling and while packing for one of his trips, he came up with the idea of visiting the countries where his clothes were made, meeting and talking to the people who made them. His travelogue was published in 2009 as *Where Am I Wearing? A Global Tour to the Countries, Factories and People that Make Our Clothes*.

Acknowledgements

Texts

p. 11: © 2009 by Kelsey Timmerman, 2010 John Wiley & Sons, Inc; **p. 14:** from The New York Times, 18 October 2008 © 2010 The New York Times. All rights reserved. Used by permission and protected by the Copyright Laws of the United States. The printing, copying, redistribution, or retransmission of the Material without express written permission is prohibited; **p. 16:** © Thomas Hylland Erikson, Globalization: The Key Concepts, 2007 and Berg Publishers an imprint of A & C Black Publishers Ltd.; **p. 18:** © Kevin Danaher, Global Exchange, www.global exchange.org, 2007; **pp. 22–23:** © Paul Reynolds, BBC MMX; **pp. 30–31:** © Paul Collier, Oxford.

Photos/Illustrations

p. 6: Shutterstock images / © litvis (monitor); **p. 7:** A: Vario Images / India Picture, B: picture-alliance / HBVerlag / Clemens Emmler, C: Alamy: © Snappaarazzi, D: © photolibrary / Big Cheese, E: © John Harris / Report Digital, F: picturealliance / dpa; **p. 8:** © Ricardo Levins Morales; **p. 9:** www.cartoonStock.com: © Piero Tonin; **p. 10:** Shutterstock images / © Olga Zaichenko (shoe), picturealliance / © dpaReport (sweatshop); **p. 11:** 'Where am I Wearing?: A Global tour to the Countries, Factories, and People that Make Our Clothes', by Kelsey Timmermann, © 2010 John Wiley & Sons, Inc.; **p. 12:** www.cartoonStock.com: © Stan Eales (cartoon), © iStockphoto / Jitalia17 (jeans); **p. 13:** © 2006 Shadowcatcher Entertainment LLC. All rights reserved; **p. 14:** Alamy: © NetPics; **p. 15:** www.cartoonStock.com: © Nigel Sutherland; **p. 16:** © Chet Phillips; **p. 17:** © laif (tower), © Andrea Mohin / New York Times / Redux / laif (airport), © iStockphoto / jurden (bird), © photolibrary / Imagesource (Delayed), © NASA / FACET (air traffic USA), © photo library / Dennis MacDonald (power plant); **p. 18:** Petra Eberhard Grafik Design, Berlin; **p. 19:** top: Associated Press (AP Photo): © Jens Meyer, middle: picture-alliance / © dpa-Report / Arno Burgi, bottom: © Reuters / Str Old; **p. 20:** © 2006 SASI Group (University of Sheffield) and Mark Newman (University of Michigan); **p. 21:** A: © XIX Commonwealth Games Delhi 2010, B: © iStockphoto / nyul, C: Gettyimages / AFP: © Cris Bouroncle, D: © UN Photo / Mark Garten; **p. 22:** Gettyimages: © Peter Macdiarmid; **p. 25:** www.cartoonStock.com: © Dave Carpenter; **p. 26:** Alamy © F. Bettex – Mysterra.org; **p. 27:** Alamy: © Stuart Forster India; **p. 28:** Alamy: © Gala Studio; **p. 29:** Alamy: © Imagestate Media Partners Limited – Impact Photos; **p. 30:** Associated Press (AP Photo): © Mauricio Piffer; **p. 33:** Shutterstock images / © Bianda Ahmad Hisham; **p. 34:** www.cartoonStock.com: © Tom Prisk; **p. 35:** www.cartoonStock.com: © Ron Morgan; **p. 44:** top: © 'The Commonwealth at 60' logo reproduced by permission of the Commonwealth Secretariat, bottom: Shutterstock images / © tatniz; **p. 45:** top: © International Monetary Fund (IMF), middle: © Ärzte ohne Grenzen e.V., bottom: © Oxfam Deutschland e.V.; **p. 46:** top: © United Nations (UNO), middle: © World Bank, Washington, DC, bottom: © World Trade Organization; **p. 47:** © Global Exchange Gallery (Danaher), Associated Press (AP Photo): © Eduardo Di Baia (Diana), Associated Press (AP Photo): © Murad Sezer (Dink), © Paul Paiewonsky / Scanpix (Eriksen), © ddp images / dapd / Axel Schmidt (Miliband), © ddp images / dapd / Jens Schlueter (Politkovskaya), © Kelsey Timmerman (Timmerman).

Cover: Corbis: © Kacper Pempel / Reuters

Map (inside back cover): Dr. Volkhard Binder, Berlin